Dancing with Snowmen

PERRY STONE

Dancing with Snowmen

DANCING WITH SNOWMEN
Published by Voice of Evangelism Outreach Ministries
P. O. Box 3595
Cleveland, TN 37320-3595
423.478.3456
www.voe.org

Scripture quotations marked KJV are from the King James Version of the Bible.

Scripture quotations marked NJKV are from the New King James Version of the Bible. Copyright © 1979, 1980, 1982 by Thomas Nelson, Inc., publishers. Used by permission.

First Edition 2013

ISBN 978-0-9785920-2-8

CONTENTS

INTRODUCTION

*"Then Jesus called a little child to Him, set him in
the midst of them, and said, "Assuredly, I say to you,
unless you are converted and become as little children,
you will by no means enter the kingdom of heaven.
Therefore whoever humbles himself as this little child is
the greatest in the kingdom of heaven. Whoever receives
one little child like this in My name receives Me."*

—Matthew 18:2-5 (NKJV)

I f the title of this book seems rather unique, blame it on an early morning dream during a Labor Day weekend. Having written over seventy books and booklets during my years of ministry, I have discovered two factors that push creativity out of a writer like toothpaste from a tube: perspiration and inspiration.

Perspiration comes when your mind goes as blank as a new sheet of paper, sending you into mental travail, in order to birth the nuggets of illumination that connect the dots along the path of spiritual insight. Inspiration, by Biblical definition, means "breathed upon by God." This was the method employed by the Holy Spirit when the prophets were inspired to dip their quills into fresh ink, and inscribe the words from God onto kosher parchments (2 Tim. 3:16). Sometimes there is a third and often untapped well that produces springs of water from the fountain of inspiration. That is the inspiration released in a spiritual dream, which is where this book title and theme originated.

On this particular Labor Day, much of Tennessee was covered with gray, slow moving clouds, almost like a scene from an Alfred Hitchcock movie. Our city of Cleveland had received a record amount of rain in twenty-four hours as a band of tropical storms crept in from the south.

The outdoor grilling plans were cancelled, so I chose to spend a few hours working on a new book to be released through the ministry. Inspiration flowed and I wrote with such ease that I began to thank the Lord for blanketing my mind with His thoughts.

Twelve hours later, at two o'clock in the morning, I suggested to my brain that it rest for a while so my flesh could get some sleep. I lay down and mumbled a prayer to keep from awakening my wife from her coma-like sleep, and asked the Lord to give me something from *His* heart that was a fresh and important word for His people.

About five-thirty in the morning I had a dream. While I cannot recall the dream, I do recall something that was said to me in the dream. I heard these words: "dancing with snowmen." Then I heard the following: "My children have forgotten how to live and walk in childlike faith. They have complicated Christianity with forms, rituals and self-preservation techniques, but they have forgotten that all blessings are released to those who have the faith of a child."

I immediately awoke and knew that this was not an idle thought from an overly worked imagination. It was a truth the Holy Spirit was expressing. I told my tired body to get up and write down these words, lest they slip away from my mind after I fell back to sleep.

When I sat down in my office next to the bedroom, those few moments turned into an hour as I filled a yellow pad with pages of notes that touched my own heart and brought back a flood of pleasant memories from my childhood.

The thoughts began with this. The teachings of Christ were *so simple that even a child could receive them*. Receiving the gift of eternal life requires three easy things: *believe* upon Christ, *repent* of your sins, and *confess* Him as your Savior (Rom. 10:10). It's a simple process that works anywhere in the world. Yet, after nineteen hundred years, churches split hairs over theological questions such as: can a saved person ever lose their salvation? What formula must be spoken over me when I'm baptized? Jesus's name only, or the name of the Father, Son and Holy Spirit? Should I be sprinkled or immersed? Is a church baptistery as acceptable as running water?

Over the centuries, the simplicity of the first century faith has become complex theology that has created division and confusion.

Church customs, traditions, and differing interpretations of Scripture have made the road to entering the kingdom rocky and confusing, rather than smooth and easy. I imagine sinners looking at our stained glass windows and wondering if the people inside the walls realize there is a world of lost, wandering souls outside their doors. Those outside aren't sure how to get past the polished greeters who hand out bulletins that announce activities to keep the sheep connected, while also preventing them from fellowshipping with the sheep in other pastures. These same outsiders are often uncertain if Christ's professed followers really believe what they are hearing, because when they exit the doors, some of them act privately in ways that are contrary to words they say "amen" to in public.

In Matthew 23:13 and 15, Jesus warned the Pharisees:

> *"But woe to you, scribes and Pharisees, hypocrites! For you shut up the kingdom of heaven against men; for you neither go in yourselves, nor do you allow those who are entering to go in."*

> *"Woe to you, scribes and Pharisees, hypocrites! For you travel land and sea to win one proselyte, and when he is won, you make him twice as much a son of hell as yourselves."*

In local churches, children's church is different from adult church. First of all, children have childlike faith, while adults often have weak faith and act like spoiled children. One word that describes the difference is *simplicity*. Children may not be mature on an emotional level, but a child can make the complicated simple. Children stick to the basics. Adults want steak and a baked potato, but children are content with peanut butter and jelly. Adults want a four course dinner, but children are happy with chicken nuggets. We enjoy our time alone, while children are always asking us to allow their friends to come over. We worry about the next paycheck. They are excited about their birthday next month.

You might say, "Children are happy because they are carefree and unbound by the problems and distractions of this world." This is certainly true in most cases. Their childlike faith doesn't see the winter of gloomy discontent that we face nearly every day. Yet, until we get back to seeing the world as simply as they do, we will never be totally free from the distracting snowdrifts that restrain our spiritual and emotional progress.

This book is for everyone who wants to return to a Christianity of joy, and untie the knots of complication and religious rituals that bind us and blind us from the joy of our salvation. When I realized that these insights were an answer to my prayer, I wrote the essence of this book in four days. I did not encounter the perspiration from mental blocks. I simply typed as fast as my fingers could fly, feeling the same inspiration and excitement that a person discovers when experiencing a "God moment" for the first time.

Within the pages of this book are stories, observations, and liberating lessons that will help you recall the dreams you have forgotten. This book will help you recover your formerly crystal-clear perception of simple faith—the faith that you experienced when you first came to Christ as a newly-born Christian.

Let these pages be a treasure map that guides you back to the delightful simplicity of being a Believer. These lessons from childhood, the reminders of the fun times, and the plain expressions and creative thinking of a child, can be lessons that open your eyes to the good things—those special presents that God has for His children. With a simple, childlike faith, nothing is impossible.

This book kept me writing, despite the rain. And I believe it can help you overlook those gray, low hanging clouds that seem to darken your plans, as you rediscover imagination and childlike faith. We can look past the snowdrifts that keep us stuck in our complicated ruts and routines, until we finally see ourselves dancing with snowmen.

Receive renewed faith,
Perry Stone, Jr.

CHAPTER 1

COCA COLA, SNOWMEN, AND MEMORIES

B efore we understand how to dance with snowmen, let's look at the history and influence of the world's most popular soft drink, Coca Cola. Have you ever wondered why Coke, as it is now known, is so popular worldwide? The known ingredients are simple and include carbonated water, a sugar product, caffeine, and spices that are used to create syrup that is considered a trade secret.

The drink was invented in May 1886 by John Pemberton, a pharmacist from Atlanta, Georgia. It was originally formulated in a three-legged brass kettle in his back yard. Pemberton planned to sell the drink at the soda fountain in his pharmacy.

Coca Cola historians say that, on average in the first year, nine servings of the drink were sold daily. Pemberton's profit the first year was a whopping fifty dollars, while his expenses for the ingredients totaled seventy dollars. It was not a good investment in the late 1800s. The drink was advertised as a tonic with medicinal properties, and the original formula contained a slight amount of cocaine from coca leaves. But that was removed from the ingredients around 1905. The drink has gone from nine glasses sold each day in 1886, to more than 1.7 billion drinks sold per day worldwide.[1]

There are two definite keys to Coke's success: a *secret ingredient* and *marketing*. One of the most intriguing aspects of Coke is the list of secret ingredients that make up the syrup and create the taste of the product. Since the beginning, these ingredients have been a well-guarded trade secret. The formula was purchased by Asa Chandler, an early president of the Coca Cola Company, who desired to maintain secrecy so that no competitor could copy the taste, since other drink companies were producing their own beverages. There is something called "merchandise 7X" that gives Coke its unique flavor.

According to historian and author Mark Pendergrast in his book, *For God, Country and Coke*, there are only two living people—who never fly on the same plane, just in case the plane crashes—that know the secret recipe. The secret is also stored in a bank vault in Atlanta, Georgia. This mysterious secret recipe has kept the Coke tradition alive for generations.

However, Coke's key to success could be more than its product. In an interview which aired on the History channel, Coca Cola executives said they believe the product's real success is found in its incredible marketing methods. The marketing director said that Coca Cola's advertising connects Coke with happy and pleasant memories while families grew up drinking Coca Cola. The Coca Cola seal with the red and white script has never changed from its beginning. This allows global recognition of the product in any country or language for generations. You need not speak English to know you are drinking Coca Cola; just look at the bottle or can. It was the idea of using *memories* connected to Coke that gained my attention.

I have seen Coca Cola memorabilia from the time I can remember. We even had one of those five-cent, glass bottle, red Coke machines in the basement of our rural church in Big Stone Gap, Virginia in the mid-1960s. The Coke Company marketed this single product using posters, trays, calendars, postcards, and any other visual stimuli that created a good memory. Often they used the image of a child, or a woman or man with a big smile on their faces, holding a bottle of Coca Cola. One image was of a young boy fishing next to his grandfather, while sipping on a Coke. There were images of young women from the twenties, dressed in ruffles and carrying brightly colored umbrellas, holding a bottle of Coke.

And who can forget the boy with his dad, eating a hot dog at a baseball game, and holding a refreshing, cold Coca Cola?

The images are almost endless, but they were carefully designed by marketing experts to connect happy memories with Coca Cola. This helped maintain Coke drinkers from one generation to the next. As times have changed, so have the images. But the old pictures are still a favorite, and they still trigger mental images of earlier times, when family life was simple and enjoyable.

COCA COLA AND SANTA CLAUS

Here is part of Coke's history that some people are not aware of. It was marketing experts at Coca Cola who first created the image of the man who is today recognized globally as Santa Claus. To be fair, there was a real man named Nicholas who was born in the third century on the southern coast of Turkey in a city named Patara, a region which was then under the control of Greece. Nicholas was raised in a religious family that taught him Christianity.[2]

His parents died when he was young. In obedience to the words of Christ in Matthew 19:21 to sell what you have and give to the poor, Nicholas took his inheritance and began to travel throughout the countryside and assist the poor. He was later assigned to be Bishop of Myra and was known throughout the region as a caring and generous man who loved children and would do anything to help the needy. Numerous stories and traditions have been handed down for generations about Saint Nicholas, but especially stories about how he would surprise the poor by secretly providing bags of gold to meet their needs. A tradition emerged that, at times, Nicholas would throw a bag of gold in a window and it would land in a shoe or on a stocking. Thus began the tradition of hanging your stocking on the fireplace mantle.

In the Catholic and Orthodox tradition, Saint Nicholas is said to be the patron saint who protects children, thus the link between Saint Nick and children receiving gifts on Christmas.[3]

A book was written in the 1800s by the famous English novelist Charles Dickens called, *A Christmas Carol*. The popularity of his novel spread from England to America, providing inspiration and a new interest in

Christmas as a special season of spending time with family, exchanging gifts, and helping the poor.

In an 1862 edition of Harper's Weekly, Thomas Nast, a Civil War cartoonist, first created a drawing of the character now recognized as Santa Claus. He sketched a short, elf-like figure that supported the Northern Union armies. For the next thirty years, Nast changed the color of Santa's coat, the hats, and the physical size of the character. Eventually he changed the traditional tan coat for a bright red one. So why has the traditional, red-suited, white-bearded Santa image remained in the American culture for the past hundred years? You could say that Coca Cola marketing played an important role.

Starting in 1931, Coke introduced advertisements by artist Haddon Sundblom, including one of a jolly-looking, pleasantly plump man sporting a white beard and a red suit, sitting by a small train under a Christmas tree, with a bottle of Coca Cola in his hand. This image appeared in magazines for three decades, while the paintings used on posters, trays, calendars, and magazines found their way across the nation and then the world.

Soon Coca Cola became associated with what is traditionally the most joyful time of the year— Christmas. Since Coke had been advertised as a refreshing summer drink, the Coke marketers want to create an image that Coke was good all season long—including winter. Linking Coke with Santa created the image that Coke is as good in the winter as it is in the summer. The idea caught on and the combination worked.

Numerous original paintings of Coca Cola Santas are stored in the archives of the company headquarters in Atlanta, Georgia. The images were so loved that, on one occasion, when the artist failed to place a wedding ring on Santa's finger, people wrote letters to the Coke headquarters asking what had happened to Mrs. Claus.[4]

By now I'm sure you are asking what this story has to do with faith, or even the faith of a child. First, for a moment, please set aside your personal opinion about whether or not it is appropriate to celebrate Christmas, or if you believe that Christ was most likely born during one of the fall feasts. Instead of arguing over an issue that has no bearing on a person's redemptive covenant (as Christ's death and resurrection is the entrance point for redemption), look for a moment through the eyes of a child and ask yourself why, with their parents approval, do children climb into the lap of a complete stranger at a mall, and one who is wearing a red coat and a white beard, at that?

The simple answer is that they are asking for a gift for Christmas. However, look beyond the simple answer to this fact: *their young lives are consumed with imagination and with experiencing happy moments; and for them, this is a happy moment.*

When we mature and become adults, those childlike imaginations that could carry us from our living room to distant lands are overcome with negative images such as the possibility of a recession, fear of joblessness, or fear of a physical problem that just might be cancer. Our God-given imagination that once could picture Jesus walking on water or feeding a hungry multitude, has now been suppressed by rational thinking that destroys our faith and explains away the miraculous.

"I believe" has been replaced with, "Why Lord?" The mustard seed faith that was promised to move mountains (Matt. 17:20) is crushed under the weight of a mountain of negative personal circumstances. We have lost the simple, childlike manner of *seeing the invisible and believing the impossible,* and our minds have become cluttered with years of discouragement, fear, and problems. The candle of illumination has been snuffed out and the darkness of doubt has replaced the light of faith. We prayed prayers that were not answered the way we expected—or were not answered at all—and then we built a theology to accommodate a tragedy instead of continuing to believe, despite the tragedy.

Life comes in seasons, we are told. Spring is our youth, which brings newness of life, hope, and planning. Summer is the time to cultivate relationships as we watch our family grow. Fall is a season of harvest when we begin to reap the benefits from our hard work. Eventually we approach winter, where warmth turns to cold, light slowly dims, and the sun begins to settle on life. Winter is often viewed as a metaphor for the closing days of a person's life. This analogy is pointed out in Paul's final letter, written to his spiritual son Timothy, when he told him to do all diligence to get to him before winter—not just before the cold set into the cobblestone floors and rock-walled dungeon of the Roman prison, but before the cessation of his earthly life (2 Tim. 4:9). You may dread the coming of winter, but children do not. And neither did Jesus!

You have probably read it, but read right over it. Notice one verse found in John 10:22: "Now it was the Feast of Dedication in Jerusalem, and it was winter." The winter season in Jerusalem runs from December through February, although December tends to be milder, while the colder weather overshadows the city in January and February. Jesus was celebrating a feast called the Feast of Dedication, in winter. This Feast of Dedication was also called the "Festival of Lights," and today it is known as Hanukkah. This is a yearly Jewish celebration commemorating the revolt against and defeat of the army of Antiochus Epiphanes by a group of Jews called the Maccabees. They ran the enemy out of the Temple and restored Jewish worship to the true Jewish priests.

There was only enough oil left to light the Temple's golden candelabra for one day; but the oil supernaturally lasted for eight days, long enough for more oil to be properly prepared and given to the priest. The festival celebrates this defeat, the supernatural miracle, and the rededication of the altar in the Temple.

During Hanukkah, Jewish families prepare certain foods, and the children play special games. Over time, they began to give the children a gift each day of the celebration. Hanukkah is a Jewish celebration that nearly coincides with the Christmas celebration; in fact, on the Hebrew calendar, the first day of Hanukkah always begins on the 25th day of Kislev[5,6]. So, we see that both the Jews and Christians have distinct celebrations that come in winter and begin on December 25, although the Hanukkah dates will vary each year on the secular calendar. The Jews celebrate the light of the menorah that supernaturally remained lit for eight days, while the Christians celebrate the Light of the world who remains the Light to this day.

For many children, winter means that snow could be in the forecast. Snow also paints the image of school cancellations, indicating they can spend the day dressed in coats and boots, and hit the yard playing in white stuff that looks like bits of cotton candy falling from heaven. We adults might think the snow is beautiful, but we no longer enjoy playing in it. That's for the kids. We don't want to get cold and damp. We hope the snow goes away quickly so we won't have to spend days or weeks driving in it and shoveling it.

The older we get, the more negatively we perceive things—even things we once enjoyed. We will take a warm shower and jump in a cold swimming pool, but we don't want to get wet when it rains. It is water either way; just a different set of circumstances. We will take a week of vacation to walk on a beach, perspire in the heat, and shop until we drop. Yet when we drive around town, the windows are up and the air conditioner is on.

Children who were raised in the Western Hemisphere, in a home that understands American traditions and customs, know that winter also means Christmas is coming in December. Most Americans, even those who reject the idea of Christ being the Savior, still enjoy the season and cannot always explain why. I have seen many Christmas seasons come and go in my lifetime, and I have observed one thing: attitudes of people change during the Christmas season. People treat others differently during this time. Folks tend to be friendlier, more talkative, kinder, and warmer to other people during this time of year. Why is this? I believe there are several reasons that are important to this discourse.

The first undeniable fact is that, despite the commercialization of the season, Christmas holds pleasant and happy memories for a vast majority of people who celebrate the season. They decorate their homes with lights and bake foods they might not enjoy at other times of the year. The scent of spices and freshly baked cookies warms the air. Churches bring out the old Christmas carols we have heard since childhood, and the sanctuary is scattered with visitors who make their annual pilgrimage to church to watch their children or grandchildren perform in a Christmas play or children's choir.

Personally, my fondest memories for almost forty years were of visiting my grandparent's home in West Virginia for Christmas. For months I anticipated the long trip to Davis, which was said to be the highest incorporated town east of the Rockies. A quiet and quaint community of a few hundred residents, the townspeople saw thousands of tourists pass through each year. This is where memories were made with my parents, grandparents, siblings, and cousins.

It was always a joyful occasion, and my grandmother cooked for days in preparation for our arrival. I thought she could have won any cooking contest, especially with her homemade vegetable soup. Granddad had his favorite recliner. And when he entered the room, anybody resting comfortably in his chair knew in advance that they should get up and move before he kindly informed them to sit elsewhere.

We stayed up late, as the cold wind whistled a winter tune across the window panes and huge snowflakes blanketed the community like a cloud descending from heaven. We could just about guarantee there would be snow for Christmas—usually a foot or two, at least. In the evenings after dinner, we sat around a dining table and played Scrabble, Acquire, and other mentally challenging games. Family members from around the area stopped in to visit and enjoy the great fellowship and food.

When Christmas day arrived we all—as many as sixteen people—squeezed our way in a small living room where gifts were piled around a tree. With three ministers in the room, there was no struggle finding one to read the nativity story from Luke's Gospel, and then offer a prayer of thanksgiving for sending Jesus Christ, a person whom everyone in the small room acknowledged as their Redeemer.

Then began the handing out of gifts. Granddad Bava would sit in a wooden dining chair, always near the hallway. He came prepared with two things—a sharp knife to cut the ribbon and paper from his gifts, and a large garbage bag to deposit the remains of the paper. I can still see his smile and hear that jolly laugh when something struck his funny bone, especially when he opened a crazy gift someone had chosen especially for him.

The ladies prepared a meal fit for a king, and we feasted in the afternoon and ate leftovers throughout the evening. The featured meat was a well-prepared turkey, and sometimes I was selected to carve the bird and place it on the serving tray.

When we were children, we played for hours in the snow until we returned home nearly frozen, like the long icicles hanging from the gutters. We rode sleds, had snowball fights, and created snow angels on the ground. And of course, no fresh snowfall would be complete without building a snowman. This was a task all of us kids took on from time to time, and my goal was to have the best looking snowman in town.

DANCING WITH SNOWMEN

As a child, I was giddy with excitement when I anticipated building this snowman. We all joined forces and rolled snowballs into boulders. The holiday song, "Frosty the Snowman," always came to mind. The lyrics spoke of an ordinary snowman that came to life when a special hat was placed on his head. As silly as the lyrics sound to an adult, we children must have thought it was perfectly *believable* that round balls of snow could move, speak, sing, and dance. Children think *anything* is possible. Maybe that is why the song has remained popular over time; it takes adults back to a happy thought, when the creativity of make-believe brought a smile to our faces and a laugh to our hearts.

Humming that tune in my mind, I would pick out the perfect spot for my own Frosty and roll the first boulder in place. Then, as the others put their hands into the task, we would fashion a second, slightly smaller ball, and heave the round chunk on top of the first. Finally, like an amateur echo of God's first created man, we sculpted a head, carved a place for his eyes, inserted a carrot for the nose, and when available, strategically placed a few small lumps of coal—West Virginia's black gold—onto his face to create a smile. Once I helped myself to one of Granddad's hats to top off the snowman's appearance, which was not one of my better ideas, as that was the hat he wore to church.

Once the snowman was finished, we stood back, admired our creation, and jumped around in a childish dance. Though we did not *speak* our friend into existence, we knelt on the ground and *formed* him from snow with our own hands. We ignored our wet gloves, the biting cold wind, and the effort it took to roll and lift heavy balls of snow. We simply believed that we could make the imaginable tangible. And that childhood game of make-believe (which was blind to everything but our imagination), brought into our dimension something that had never existed before—our latest version of Frosty the snowman.

So why is Christmas special to so many people? Because of the *happy memories*!

In a world filled with suffering, pain, death, famine, wars and grief, we need more happy times and thoughts. The season is also cheery because it is the one time of year that people, for a brief window of time, stop concentrating on themselves and, instead, think about the needs or desires of other people. Think about the hours people spend shopping for that one unique gift that will cause the recipient to smile with delight and offer a kiss or a hug in return.

Maybe there is a message in all of this. Why can't the spirit of joyfulness and the desire to help others that we feel at Christmas exist all year long in the Kingdom of God? I am not speaking of the traditional celebration of keeping lights in the windows or decorations in your living room all year long. I am referring to the same spirit that children have when they anticipate the season and look forward to the good times with family, and when they use their uninhibited imagination to build a snowman and dance with excitement at their creation. As grownups, we lose that sense of anticipation.

Since April 2, 1982 my wonderful wife Pam and I have been married. She plans our vacation a year in advance to ensure that I don't book every weekend for a preaching engagement or a conference. She loves family time, and she *anticipates* vacation a year in advance. She loves to take pictures on vacation. Once I asked her why she took so many pictures and she said, "We're making memories." She loves to make memories and keep track of them with pictures. I can attest to that because we have a cabinet full of memories in the form of pictures she has taken since 1982. Each photo captured a moment in time that cannot be relived or altered. We have wedding pictures, taken at the Northport Church of God in Northport, Alabama, of a lovely young woman in a flowing white wedding dress and a nervous, skinny, black-haired, twenty-three-year-old young man in a white tuxedo, when suddenly…a flash from a camera captured an unforgettable memory. Pamela Taylor, at that very moment in her life, gave up her last name to become Mrs. Pamela Stone, and the covenant was sealed by a kiss from yours truly.

HAPPY MEMORIES

Snowmen are created in the cold and they melt in the heat. They originate with the snow that falls from the heavens, but they melt and disappear onto the earth as water. They were formed by small hands using their minds and creativity. Eventually, all that remains is a happy *memory* of what was. Can you remember your snowman—an image that represents life when things were simple, when stress did not exist, and when people worked together to accomplish something and had fun doing it? When winter was not dreaded, cold was expected, and snowmen were welcomed?

Happy memories—the secret that has kept millions of people buying Coca Cola for generations—is also one of the secrets to anticipation. Have we lost something here? How do we get it back, when the winter storms are blowing away the comfort zone of our faith? Christ said that children make up the Kingdom of heaven. So what lessons can we learn from a child? Can we grow older and still have fun? Yes we can, if we again tap into the one characteristic all children have that makes life interesting: imagination.

CHAPTER 2

MAKE BELIEVE

It's the spark of creativity that fuels every childhood dream. It turns a boy's bedtime blanket into an unexplored cave, and the little girl's stuffed animals into guests at a tea party. *Imagination* brings storybook characters to life, and walks children through a virtual garden of ideas that exists only in their minds.

God used His imagination to create everything from nothing that could be seen (Heb. 11:3). He then created us in His image, and gave us a creative imagination that allows us to make something out of next to nothing. From birth, God implanted within us imagination and creativity.

With just a spoken word, the Creator turned an infinite void into an ever-expanding universe. Giving voice to His imagination, He ignited the inferno of countless stars, and sent planets spinning into orbit. Like an inspired painter doodling on a three-dimensional canvas, God sketched out continents and colored the oceans with the brush of mere words. God brought life—to life!

"Let there be grass."

And with the echo of His voice, a carpet of green grass covered the earth.

"Let there be trees."

And forests of foliage sprouted, decorating the planet with all kinds of trees, some bearing fruit.

"How about some birds and fish…." And suddenly a convoy of wings blanketed the sky and schools of fish splashed among the waves.

With little effort, God's creative imagination turned the ethereal void into something that had never before existed—a dimension that could be touched. He made the imaginable tangible. Then building on that solid foundation, God Himself eventually knelt on the freshly formed earth and stuck His hands into the mud.

And God said, "Let us make man in our image, after our likeness…" (Gen 1:26).

And the Lord God formed man of the dust of the ground, and breathed into his nostrils the breath of life; and man became a living soul" (Gen. 2:7).

The Creator did not speak man into existence as He did the burning stars and spinning planets. He *made* him from the earth. With His own hands He sculpted eyes, ears, nose, and toes. He crafted the four chambers of man's heart, the weave of his hair, and the ridges of his brain. Bending down, the Creator exhaled the breath of life into that first man of clay, filling his lungs with air, his mind with knowledge and creativity, and his soul with the same imagination that had created him.

God saw the intangible and spoke it into existence. Then He fashioned us to display the same creativity. We each have written within us the ability to make the imaginable tangible.

Despite that divine inheritance imprinted into the very DNA of God's first human child, we as adults rarely entertain the childlike creativity of blind faith. Why not? What has caused us to discount our God-given abilities to create by faith what we cannot see by sight?

It is as though a wedge has been placed between our mind's intellect and our spirit's inspiration. Somewhere along the way, we divided the notion of blind faith into two separate and conflicting ideas—blind, meaning the inability to see; and faith, meaning the evidence of things not seen (Heb. 11:1).

Our logic as an adult has rendered us incapable of seeing the invisible that we knew was there as a child. We can no longer imagine the space beneath a child's bedtime blanket as an adventure-filled cave to be explored. As adults, we see a dark room and a blanket.

Children see no limitations; adults perceive limitations as inescapable. The imaginary tea parties have been replaced by the down-to-earth preparation for our next meal. In our unimaginative world, our logic has turned us into "old fuddy-duddies" who are stuck in the mud and mire of maturity.

But from a lifeless and dark void, God created the entire universe. And if He can speak and make something out of that, imagine what He can make out of each of us if we will listen.

> *"At the same time came the disciples unto Jesus, saying, Who is the greatest in the kingdom of heaven? And Jesus called a little child unto him, and set him in the midst of them, and said, Verily I say unto you, Except ye be converted, and become as little children, ye shall not enter into the kingdom of heaven. Whosoever therefore shall humble himself as this little child, the same is greatest in the kingdom of heaven."*
> *— Matt. 18:1-4 (KJV)*

Christ's words and illustrated messages were so simple that a child could understand them. But His message was intended for all of those clay-men among us.

We must become like children again, and once more learn how to view our world as a creation of wonder. We must gaze at our surroundings like Adam did when he was newly formed, and when he awoke and saw Eden for the first time. Like a child, we must be open to God's unseen provision, and live as if we are perpetually dining at a tea party that only we can see. To return to that childhood perspective, we must be willing to step into the unexplored caves and rediscover the adventurous faith that we lost.

Blind faith is not the failure to see what is possible, but rather the possibility of seeing everything except failure. It's the way most of us saw the world in our childhood. In childhood, we did not understand the world of limitations when we played with friends. The back yard was the world, and we could choose the nation we were in.

Winter was always my favorite season of the year, but not because I enjoyed cold weather. I enjoyed it because of the potential for snow. A few inches of snow on the ground meant a time of creating. As children, we were always ready to make-believe. We made-believe that the snowballs were cannon balls that could knock down the wall of a castle. If there was enough snow, the igloo fort was always popular with the guys. Whatever we did in the snow, the cold was insignificant because our time outside was simple and pure.

Thinking back on my childhood, it doesn't take a game of spiritual Scrabble to see that the words *make* and *believe* belong together. From the Garden of Eden, when Adam named the animals, to the backyard of my grandparent's home in Davis, West Virginia, the creations we make and the Creator we believe in are connected.

Adam was dust on the ground, until God's creative mind released an image and created from dust a living soul. Then kneeling on the ground of Eden, God formed an image of Himself with His own hands (Gen. 1:27, 2:7). Man did not exist until God released what He imagined.

In a similar manner, the snowman did not exist until we first envisioned him. And once we saw him in our mind, he became a reality in our hands.

In both cases, our visions were realized in the same way that a child plays make-believe. Most adults think this is just a trivial game that children play to pass the time. But if we pay attention to the words of Jesus, it becomes clear that, in the eyes of a child (just as in the spirit) things happen in a different order.

If you make-believe, then you are just pretending. But if you believe and then make, you are creating.

CHAPTER 3

YOU'VE GROWN UP AND FORGOTTEN HOW TO FLY

One of the warmest memories I have of my son Jonathan when he was growing up happened before he started to school, while I was preaching a revival in North Carolina. He was a blond-haired, blue-eyed little angel who was (and still is) my pride and joy. Our time together was always after the night services, when he and I would stay up playing games, talking, or watching a children's movie. My wife had purchased a movie called Hook. Jonathan enjoyed this movie and asked me to watch it with him every night after church for an entire week. By the time the week was over, I could quote the lines in the movie before they were spoken.

Hook was a story of how Peter Pan grew up and his children were kidnapped by Captain Hook, thus forcing Peter to return to never-never land to rescue his children. The central theme in the movie, at least to me, was this: When the grown-up Peter was the youthful Peter Pan, he used his imagination to create food from nothing. He could fly by thinking happy thoughts. As Peter Pan, he would fly in the air to London from never-never land, and eventually he fell in love and married. As he settled into his life in London, the cares of life and the desire to make money overtook his family life. Eventually, Peter Pan became Peter the businessman and he forgot how to fly.

On his rescue mission, he returned to the lost boys and to his friends from earlier years. These children of various ages had to change Peter's way of thinking, forcing him to use his imagination and remember how to be young again. Once Peter's happy thoughts returned, he remembered how to fly, which enabled him to rescue his children and return them home to London.

Yes, I know that people cannot fly except in their dreams at night, when they flail their hands and kick their feet and lift themselves into the air, only to wake up and find that they are lying on a hard mattress staring into the dark. But there is an application from this popular movie that we adults should consider.

We grow up in this calloused, competitive, fast-paced world where every Monday begins another week of work. We arrive at eight o'clock and give the company eight or more hours of our life each day, which in turn helps us maintain the needs of life—a roof over our heads, an automobile, food, and necessities for the family. In the process, we are often so bogged down with the cares of life that we forget how to fly. We forget how to enjoy the simple things in life that brand unforgettable memories in our minds. Our children beg us to play with them, but the chains of work hold us in the office working overtime. Our children want us to play games, but our body is dragging and telling us, maybe another day. The next day we return to work in a rut, and any promise we have made to our children fades until it disappears.

If you are thirty years of age right now, look forward about forty years into the future to your retirement. Hopefully, you have built a nest egg, are comfortable in your retirement, and thankful for those many days of overtime that are now paying off. Finally you can sleep in, enjoy vacations, and spend time with those children that you didn't have time for while they were growing up. The freedom of retirement has provided the chance to *fly* with those you love. The ropes that tied you to work are long gone, and now you control your destiny. Time is your friend, and you have plenty of it.

You call your children and ask them to come over for dinner. But they are working overtime and dinner won't fit in their busy schedule. You suggest a weekend cookout at your place. But their company has planned a staff retreat for that same weekend. When your children wanted to fly, you forgot how. And now that you can fly, there is nobody to fly with you. Perhaps they are living what they saw while growing up—that money and work are more important than time with the family.

When I was a fiery traveling evangelist in my twenties, I preached in churches where the ministers were ten to fifteen years from retirement. These men gave me advice such as, stay humble, preach the Word, never retaliate against your adversaries, love the church. Those closest to retirement offered one consistent piece of advice that went something like this: *"You are young now, but time will pass quickly. Before you know it, you will be my age and near retirement. When you have children, you will blink your eyes and suddenly they will be grown. Son, stay close to God, your wife and your children, because as you approach the end, they will be all that you will have."*

In my twenties I sported a headful of black hair and a mustache. There was not one wrinkle on my face and I could preach for weeks at a time without taking a break. I was not invincible, but I was energized.

Then it happened. Gray sidewalls began to overtake my black hair like weeds in a garden. Crow's feet around my eyes followed shortly thereafter, and a turkey neck emerged, seemingly out of nowhere. Those long revivals became three-day and five-service weekend conferences. When you are in your twenties, you know that old age is concealed in your DNA, but energy and activity keep you too busy to think about it. Eventually, daily activity slows while time and age catch up with each other. Soon you find yourself in the place those ministers talked about.

However, I don't want to have the Peter Pan syndrome, and climb up the ladder of life toward the gate to heaven, and then forget how to enjoy a little *flying*—that is, relaxation, vacations, and family time—with my wife and children.

Several years ago Pam purchased two dirt motorbikes for Jonathan and me. Occasionally I rode mine on the road, but Jonathan stayed in the yard, lacking the confidence to take his beyond the grass around the house. Later I decided to sell both bikes and get a small dune buggy for the youth ranch. This one small vehicle has been fun for my daughter and at times my son. I have watched my daughter invite a friend to put on the protective helmet and sit on the right seat as she drives the vehicle on the property behind the VOE ministry center.

Vacations demand time off from work and some extra finances, but the memories that are made and the moments captured on camera (or now, on cell phones) will be priceless. Never get too busy to fly and never fly alone.

CHAPTER 4

CHILDREN LOVE
TO IMAGINE
THE UNSEEN

Today's young people are tech savvy, with iPods, iPads, cell phones, Internet access, games online, and other forms of communication and technology that find their way into the hands of a generation that accesses information quickly and easily. One of the problems with computers is that the computer programmers have done most of the thinking for you.

When I was a young boy living in the mountains of Southwestern Virginia in the 1960s, it required a serious imagination to play any game. There were not many board games and we couldn't walk into a store and find a store full of toys like we see today. Besides, being from a lower income household and having three children in the family, we could not just go to a store and purchase anything we wanted. But we did a wonderful job at making up for this lack by tapping into *internal creativity*.

For boys, a stick became a toy gun. Dolls with homemade clothes were common for girls, and the girls used their imagination to become a nurse and treat the invisible ailments of their dolls and patients. The closet in the house became a cave, and a sheet pulled over a clothesline became an army tent. A couple of plates and forks were all we needed to organize a new restaurant offering the finest of invisible cuisine, with a friend chosen as manager of the operation. And don't forget, it was all free. Any grown-up who didn't believe the food was there would be reprimanded and told to eat the hot pizza, anyway.

In my childhood days, kids were often seen talking to themselves. This was a habit that was not easy for me to break. Even in my late teenage years, I would spend so much time alone studying that I would think out loud, since there was nobody else in the room with whom I could carry on a normal conversation. My father once asked me why I was talking out loud to myself. I replied, "I like to hear what a good man has to say," to which he began laughing hard enough to turn his white cheeks a rosy red.

Observe a child closely when they are unaware that you are watching. They will enter a world of their own by using the God-given creativity of their minds. The invisible to them suddenly becomes visible, and the visible can suddenly be ignored and become invisible. Children might even have an imaginary friend, one that only they can see.

Eventually the children grow into adulthood, and the invisible world of make-believe is replaced by the reality of a visible world, where they are surrounded by cares of this life, the deceitfulness of riches, and the lust of other things" (Mark 4:19).

As children, when we heard the stories of the Bible, *we believed every word*. We drew our pictures of stick people to illustrate what we saw in our minds, and we honestly believed that God could do anything. We expected to fly away to heaven one day and be with Jesus, as we sang a red-backed hymnal song titled, "I'll Fly Away."

Then we grew up and attended a secular university where a liberal professor spewed lectures of poisonous unbelief as he attacked the Christian faith, creationism, the supernatural, and everything you once believed. After coming close to losing our faith—if we kept it at all—we were awarded our degree and a nice secular job with a company that allowed us to meet all types of people: atheists, agnostics, Jews, Muslims, Buddhists, and men and women from nations around the world. Soon what was left of our childhood Christian faith was weakened, and we began to view religion as a hodgepodge of ancient beliefs that separated the world into religious factions, but produced little evidence of the existence of God.

Soon those simple, cherished childhood memories of sitting in a

Sunday School class and being taught the stories of the Christian faith are erased from your intellectual mainframe. The seeds of faith are now missing from the soil of your heart. Plainly and simply, you have forgotten how to believe. Your new way of thinking says, "You can't believe in the invisible. And you can't believe in the supernatural. No rational mind would believe any of that." You might even say, "There is no God, because I can't see Him, and I won't believe in anything I can't see."

Some things simply prove that God exists. If you are a husband, have you ever been present in the room when your wife gave birth to one of your children? I was present at the birth of both my son and daughter. Both times I encountered a unique experience, the memories of which have not faded with time. When I saw our children's faces for the first time, I compared the emotional feeling to the feeling I had at the moment I received Christ as a child. I understood why Christ identified the initial redemptive experience as being "born again" (John3:3). When a child is first born, there is a newness of life released on the earth as a new creation has come into being!

Evolution cannot explain the *emotion* you feel at the birth of a child, nor can it explain the *compassion* you feel when you seeing hurting people, or the hate that is replaced by love for people who have wronged you, once you enter a redemptive covenant with Christ. Look into the face of a newborn infant that has the eyes of her mother or the nose of his dad, and tell God that He does not exist.

IT'S EASIER FOR CHILDREN TO SEE THE INVISIBLE

When our son Jonathan was about six years of age, he was in the kitchen of our home when he saw a man standing in the laundry room next to the kitchen. He said to his mother, "Mommy, who is that man in there?" Pam turned to look and saw nobody in the room.

She asked, "What did you see?"

He described in detail the man, his hair, and the clothing he was wearing. For several days I would ask him what he saw and he repeated it in detail, without wavering.

Several months later Pam was outside on the deck of our house when Jonathan said, "Mommy, there he is again in the yard. Who is he?"

Again she asked, "What did you see?"

He replied, "I saw the man, but he had on a different color shirt." Pointing at the swing set, Jonathan said, "I saw him from the corner of my eye and he was there." He was not afraid when he saw this individual, and he was certain of what he had seen. Years later, when I asked him again about seeing this man, he repeated the story in detail, without any alteration. Pam and I both believe the person was an angelic being in human form (Heb. 13:2), that for some reason Jonathan was allowed to briefly see.

Even in the Bible an old donkey saw more than an old prophet! The Old Testament seer—that is, Balaam's donkey—stopped cold in his tracks when the beast saw an angel blocking the path. The eyes of this animal were opened to the spirit realm, while the man who operated in a prophetic gift was blinded to the invisible. When an animal can see what a prophet cannot, there is something missing in the vision of the prophet or preacher.

At times our eyes will be opened to what we can't ordinarily see. When Elisha arose from his morning sleep and stood on the mountain, the Assyrian army was camped at the base of the hill, planning to capture the prophet. Elisha was sensitive to the invisible spirit realm and immediately saw horses and chariots of fire surrounding him on top the mountain. Elisha's servant was blind to the angelic assistance, and only when Elisha prayed for his servant's eyes to be opened, did the servant see the invisible world of angels and spirits (2 Kings 6:17).

Children don't have to see something to believe it, but most adults won't believe something until they see it. Adults believe that you must see it before you can better understand it. Yet there are many things I see and *don't understand*. I don't understand how a black cow can eat green grass and give white milk that churns into yellow butter; but I eat the steak, drink the milk, and use the butter. I don't understand how the tiny wings of a bumble bee can carry the bee's weight and the bee can fly from flower to flower. But I believe it and so does the bee, despite the fact that scientific research says it is impossible for a bee to fly. Consider the following:

- How can a cow eat grass and produce milk, a sheep eat grass and make wool?

- How can beans grow up a pole from left to right, and morning glories from right to left?

- How can seeds planted upside down sprout right side up?

- How can watermelons always have an even number of stripes?

- How can oranges always have an even number of segments, and corn have one piece of silk for each kernel?

- How can a cat that was lost in Florida travel 3,000 miles in two and a half years, and get back to its home in California?

- How can electricity be put into one box and freeze a chicken, but electricity in another box will fry a chicken?

- How is hydrochloric acid poisonous, yet it is found in cherries, plums and peaches?

- How can the earth spin, orbit around the sun, and move with the rest of the Solar System around our galaxy, all at the same time?

- How you can blow on your hands in winter and they feel warm, yet blow on your hands in summer and they feel cool?

We don't necessarily understand some things, but they are facts nonetheless. Before you reject the idea of believing in something invisible, keep in mind that the invisible air you just inhaled contains oxygen molecules that you cannot see, but they are necessary to keep you alive. The wind is invisible but you can feel it. The wind cannot be seen, yet it can be heard whistling through the leaves.

We experience the effects of the wind's power when hurricanes strike a community. Those air molecules can formulate a dangerous natural disaster when the invisible becomes a visible hurricane. The invisible power of faith is like a strong wind, releasing visible miracles when we have faith to believe the Word of God. Our faith is the substance of things hoped for, the evidence of things not seen (Heb. 11:1). Faith will make the invisible visible and the impossible possible.

As Jesus said, "If you can believe, all things are possible to him that believes" (Mark 9:23). With childlike faith in God and His Word, anything that is His will can be accomplished—as easily as seeing nothing but snow and knowing that you can take flakes of crystalline water ice and create from it a snowman.

CHAPTER 5

CHILDREN PLAY WITH ANYONE

The problem with children is often the adults! Those grown-ups complain about this dumbed-down generation of lost youth who stay glued to their computers for long hours, sleep past breakfast, and have as much motivation as a turtle crossing a road. Those complaints turn to fears when Mom and Dad discover that their son or daughter has been pouring alcohol into their system and popping dangerous pills into their bodies.

"Why do they do it?" is the perplexing question.

The answer? Blame it on the grown-ups.

After all, who makes billions of dollars selling unlimited types of beer, wine, and wine coolers? Answer: a group of grown-ups motivated by other grown-ups who sit in boardrooms reading profit charts and patting themselves on the back as income increases from the sale of the same drinks that cause highway deaths, drunk driving arrests, prison sentences, verbal and physical abuse, and neglect of families. We can blame drug dealers who are proud of their new thirty-million-dollar yacht that was purchased with the blood money of a young person who died prematurely from illegal drugs.

Who produces the drugs and alcohol? Not the children or the teens. They are just the casualties of war, the easy purchasers of drugs using cash that benefits the demons of death who prey on innocent teens like starving mice searching for a load of cheese in the house. While the young people might pop pills and smoke weed, it is an adult who grew it or produced it; an adult who shipped it; an adult who set up the sales arrangements; and adults who stuff their pockets with the cash while your child is in intensive care hanging in a chasm between life and death.

If children have a weakness, it is that they can be gullible and too trusting of people. This is why many youth cave to pressure from peers to drink and explore the deadly world of drugs. However, this naiveté is also one of their greatest strengths that they lose as they mature and become adults. Let me show you one difference between a child and his treatment of others, and the attitude of an adult in a similar situation. If we could keep this one simple character trait and nourish it, we could change the world in one generation.

PLAYING WITHOUT A RÉSUMÉ

Picture with me a large room filled with some of the most unique games and toys made from creative toymakers around the world. A group of four-year-old children enter the room—four boys and four girls. The first thing you notice is they are all dressed in simple play clothes, nothing fancy or expensive, just the same kind of garments worn every day when a child goes out to play.

The second observation is their skin color. They represent a range of different races. What you do *not* know is that their families have different religious backgrounds. They come from Christian, Jewish, Hindu, and Muslim backgrounds. The children are told that they have the whole day to play in the room and have fun. Later they will all eat lunch together and enjoy their favorite dessert.

At first the children are timid when they enter the room. Some have their hands in their pockets. A few sit by themselves and others run to the shelves to pull down a toy that attracts their attention. As time passes, the children warm up to each other, and we see that two girls of different races are playing at a dollhouse, and soon the rest join in. They are laughing and pretending to cook their favorite food. After two hours the little fellows have their own games going on, drawing pictures and shaping figurines from dough.

Here is the point. No child is paying attention to the color of anyone else's skin. They are not asking each other how much money their family makes, what size their home is, or what kind of car their mother drives. They did not ask the question that separates entire nations from their fellow man: What religion are you?

The children played with each other without asking for anybody's résumé.

After six hours, the parents are told about the experiment. These are religious folks, extremely loyal to their own beliefs. What do you think is the first thing a strict observer of their religion might do? A normal reaction would be for the Muslim parents to immediately separate their children from the Jewish and Christian children. The devout Jew might separate his children from the Muslim or Christian children. The Hindu family might pull their children to another part of the room. And suddenly the *adults,* who felt threatened that their child might be corrupted by another religion, create a division that children would not understand at age four. At least not until the Muslim explained, "The Jews have occupied our lands and we must not get close to them." And the Hindu said, "In India, the Muslims are our enemies, so we have nothing to do with them." Perhaps a Jewish father would remind his children that intermingling with Christians is a bad idea, since we have been taught that Christians caused the holocaust.

How do I know that this could be the reaction? Simply because, in this world, the majority of wars are fought over religion. These particular religions often clash with one another, and killings are occurring in Africa, Indonesia, India, the Middle East and other nations, as religious groups fight with other religious groups, or even with others of their same religion, over differences in religious beliefs. I have been to Israel and observed firsthand the clash between the Arabs and Jews, and the hatred that is often taught in mosques and spreads to the streets, the schools, and the homes. People who say they were Christians have been guilty over the centuries as well.

Had this been a group of forty-year-old men and women in this experiment, their different skin colors would have brought a cordial discussion about safe topics—work, the weather, and so on. But if the topic had turned to religion, the warm atmosphere would have become chilled; and if arguments had ensued, the air would have become thick enough to cut with a knife.

One of the great characteristics of a child is that they are so young and tender-hearted that they have not yet learned to perfect the art of pre-judging people by their outward appearance, skin color, or religion. You never bring a personal résumé onto the playground, because that is neutral territory, and everyone is equal and welcome to come as you are.

This may be what many Christians have forgotten: *the ground is always equal at the foot of the cross.* Jesus did not come to earth to die for Christians, but for sinners. He did not call the righteous but the lost to repentance (Matt. 9:13).

Let's look back to the scene of redemption and take a closer look at who was present at the crucifixion. When reading the four Gospels, we discover a great measure of humanity represented. We know that a couple of *thieves* were on site, as both were condemned to execution along with Christ (Matt. 27:38). At the foot of the cross were a few *gamblers*, casting lots for the garments of Christ (Matt. 27:35) and hoping to win the prize of a seamless garment. There were also *faithful women*, willing to follow Christ until the end (Matt. 27:55). John was the only *disciple* found in the narrative, as the other ten disciples fled into hiding for fear.

There were the *scribes* (Matt. 27:41), who were men trained in copying parchments of the Law of Moses and other legal documents. The *Pharisees* stood mocking Him, and even the chief *priests* from the Temple mingled in the bunch (Matt. 27:41). A *black African man* named Simon from Cyrene had borne the cross to the site of the execution and was observing from nearby (Matt. 27:32). Who can forget the *Roman guards* that drove the nails in His hands and feet, eventually piercing his side with a lance (Matt. 27:54). A *rich man* named Joseph is in the story, because he permitted Christ's body to be placed in his own tomb (Matt. 27:57).

Then there is the most loyal person in any family crisis—the mother, who in this case was *Mary*—and she was faithful until the end (John 19:25). For most men, including those incarcerated, mama is always there for you, in the good times and the bad.

Let's sum up the list:

- Thieves

- Gamblers

- Faithful women

- Disciples

- Scribes

- Pharisees

- Chief priests

- Roman soldiers

- A black man

- A rich man

- Mother

- Hundreds of bystanders

Notice that there were men and women, rich and poor, religious and non-religious, various ethnic groups, and bystanders. At the base of the cross was a representation of all humanity, all with various reasons for being there. The Roman soldiers were just doing their job. Some were there to watch another Roman crucifixion. For others, they were sadly observing the death of a prophet. Pharisees were grinning and believing they were doing God's work by removing a heretic and a religious rebel from Israel. The fact is that Jesus made it easy for any person of any color, and even any religion, to meet Him at the cross.

CHRISTIANS LOVE THEIR OWN TYPES

Christ predicted that He would build His church (Matt. 16:18), and today that church has splintered into hundreds of denominations around the world, all with their emphasis upon one particular doctrinal point that separates or distinguishes them from the others. For the Lutherans it was the emphasis on justification by faith, and for the early Methodists it was holiness and the teaching of sanctification. The Pentecostal denominations emphasized the baptism in the Holy Spirit, and the later Charismatic movement initiated fresh illumination on worship. The Baptists have a strong teaching on water baptism and are traditionally Calvinist in their theology.

Have you ever noticed that each group generally fellowships with just their own group? We are told by Christ not to hide our light under a bushel, but to let it shine (Luke 11:33). Our little bushels have become our own personal ministries, our own local churches, and our own denominations. It sure is comfortable to hide with our own kind under the security of our denominational baskets.

I am a fourth generation minister and have been connected to a major denomination since my call into the ministry. One of the strengths of a denomination is the spiritual covering it provides to maintain the integrity of the church and its ministries. One of the weaknesses is the territorial and businesslike approach that often grips the system to the point that a competitive spirit emerges among members and leaders.

Years ago I was invited to participate in a regional meeting. About eighteen churches were planning to support the meeting, but the meeting never got off the ground because the ministers disagreed about whose church facility would be used to accommodate the large crowds. The other ministers were hesitant to open the gates of their pastures and allow their sheep to pass through the doors to enter another man's pasture, for fear that they might find the grass greener on the other side.

One of the dangers facing the contemporary church in North America is the emphasis on a certain kind of pre-packaged Christianity. I have heard ministers say, "We want the cream of the crop as members of our congregation." Or, "We are building our church on the business leaders in the community and reaching out to a certain economic group." When I hear this, I wonder why the ministers don't just ask for a personal résumé and a copy of the prospective member's tax return to see if they are worthy of joining their church.

If Christ had selected His twelve disciples based upon their personal résumé, most would have flunked before the paper was ever read. Christ received sinners unconditionally and changed their lives eternally.

What lessons can we learn from a child about how to accept others unconditionally? In my opinion, a simple dog may hold a key.

Years ago we lived in a neighborhood that seemed like an outdoor zoo for dogs. I didn't see many in the neighborhood during the day, but when the sun set, they were like the proverbial werewolves in the old movies that would come out at night to howl at a full moon. It would be late at night and perhaps a car would drive through the neighborhood, or the midnight train would rumble down the tracks in the distance, when suddenly it would happen. Dogs would bark and howl from every corner of the neighborhood. One night I began to imagine that they were practicing for the church choir, as some low-barking mutt was singing base, and a smaller one was yelping a little higher in the tenor position. After years of listening to this, your mind can't help but play games!

The neighborhood was also full of children, mostly aged four to ten. When they all played outdoors, it looked like a daycare convention on lunch break. One day a forlorn-looking stray dog that could have been the poster dog for the Humane Society came dragging itself down the street and dropped into a yard. A child came over and petted the pitiful fellow. Soon, like an invitation to an all-you-can-eat ice cream buffet, all the kids began running to this new stranger and surrounded the fellow, showering him with attention and love. They didn't care where he came from, what he looked like, how old he was, or the color of his fur. He was a sad dog that may have been abused and needed comfort from people.

Most adults would have run from him or sent him to a shelter where he belonged. But not the children. Some of them scurried home to search for a few leftovers to feed him, and another brought him a bowl of water. Compassion rescued this stray from a possible trip to the animal shelter, as he became the neighborhood dog that was owned by nobody but cared for by everyone.

America has tens of thousands of churches that sometimes seem more like an adult nursery with bottle-feeding, crying, and complaining Christians who have to be burped, patted on the back, and allowed to throw an occasional temper tantrum to make sure they feel good about being so well cared for. Soon we are entrenched in our own traditions and so stuck in a routine that we almost *require* an acceptable résumé from anyone who wants to join our group. They need the right skin color, the proper background, and a matching religious upbringing.

Can we please agree on one thing—those dogs?

In the time of Christ, the Jews called Gentiles dogs. Christ said that He came to the Jew first, but on one occasion He went north of Israel toward Lebanon to a region called Tyre and Sidon. A Canaanite woman approached Him and asked Him to cure her daughter of demonic oppression. Christ said that He could not "give the children's bread to the dogs." This was a term that Jews used for Gentiles; and in its original context, it was a rather contemptible term.

The woman replied, "Even the dogs get the crumbs from the master's table" (Matt. 15:21-28). The woman understood that she had no covenant authority to be asking a Jewish healer for a miracle, as she was a Canaanite and a Gentile. However, in response to His comment she basically replied, "Ok, I'll be the dog. But even a good master will give his dog a few crumbs!"

In America dogs are our pets. We feed them good food, have them groomed, and sometimes even dress them in doggie attire. But the stray, scraggly, skinny, and homely-looking ones are seldom taken as pets. Have you ever seen a homeless man on the street? Have you ever heard the way some Christians talk about them? "If he would get a job, he wouldn't need to beg. He's probably a drug addict or an alcoholic. He needs to go to the shelter. Let the government take care of him. He probably belongs in jail." Nobody *belongs* in jail. Crime and justice *place* them in jail. People who are struggling *belong* at home, with their parents or companions and children.

The Kingdom of God is made up of "jail dogs" who belong in the Kingdom of God. The Apostle Paul was continually arrested for the Gospel. Today he would make the headlines and church members would sip their lattes and recline in their easy chairs and comment, "That man needs to quit the ministry. His arrests are a reproach to the church."

That homeless Gentile dog doesn't need to be passed from shelter to shelter, but be led into the Kingdom of God. Christ's first message was, "The Spirit of the Lord is upon me because He has anointed me to preach the Gospel to the poor" (Luke 4:18). Jesus's first outreach was to the poor.

Children sure do love those poor old dogs. They don't need to know the dog's past before they show a little unconditional love toward one of God's creatures that is suffering.

From this illustration we can glean a unique lesson. Since Gentiles were called dogs in the New Testament (Mk. 7:27), then we must acknowledge that we human dogs need love, attention and care, just like that stray dog received from compassionate children in our neighborhood when they were moved to help.

People want to know if dogs go to heaven. Without a doubt, those Gentile dogs have the potential of spending eternity in their Master's house in the heavenly city. But just like a lost animal, someone must intercept the strays, and help them find the road to the Master's house.

CHAPTER 6

CHILDREN LAUGH

Unless you are a long-term partner of our ministry, you probably never had the chance to meet John Franklin Bava. He was one of the greatest storytellers I have ever known. He was also my grandfather on my mother's side of the family. When he opened his mouth, many times it would be to tell a story or a joke. He loved to laugh, and I can't recall a day that I was around him when I didn't hear him tell a joke or laugh. It must have been good medicine, as he was seldom ever sick, even with so much as a cold. He never lifted his voice in front of others in anger, and I never heard him speak ill of anyone.

When he died at age eighty-four, he passed away a few days after having surgery for a hernia that was caused by moving furniture. While granddad was lying on the hospital gurney, preparing to be wheeled away for surgery, the last thing he did was tell a joke.

The Bible says that a merry heart does good, like medicine (Prov. 17:22). Years ago I read a study that confirmed the healing power in laughter. A good laugh relaxes the muscles for up to forty-five minutes after you have a hearty laugh. Laughing decreases the stress hormones, increases the ability of the immune system to fight sickness, releases endorphins that cause a person to feel good, and increases the flow of blood to the heart.

In 1964, a Dr. Cousins was diagnosed with crippling, incurable pains. He decided to check into a place where he spent hours each day watching Candid Camera Classics, the Marx Brothers jokes, and other comedies.

He realized that ten minutes of hard laughter set him free from pain for two hours. Eventually, he laughed his way into feeling so well that he was cured of pain!

For anyone who might think that Christians are so serious that they never have fun, you haven't been to some of the churches I have preached in. Some of the funniest things happen in church. Don't be a church member who fellowships too long with the bloodline of the descendants of the children of Israel who all died in the desert because they spent all day complaining about things they couldn't change.

IT'S OKAY TO LAUGH—EVEN IN CHURCH

I have considered writing a book called, "It Could Happen Only in a Pentecostal Church." The book would be filled with true stories of bloopers and pulpit mistakes that I have personally witnessed, experienced, or heard about over the years.

Pentecostals have been accused of being too emotional in their worship. They have been known to shout amen at the preacher; and in the old days, a fellow might get happy and begin to shout and praise God by leaping or even running down an aisle. I saw something hilarious with my own eyes when I was young. In a service at an open air tabernacle in the heat of summer, a man ran across the front of the church but lost his pants in the process. He tried to continue running while bending over and attempting to pull his pants up. He ended up leaving the service and not returning, out of embarrassment I presume.

Another minister was preparing to read his text and began fumbling around for his glasses. He said to the congregation, "Now where are they?" He finally said, "I'll try to read without them." When he read his text, he suddenly shouted, "I'm healed! I'm healed!" The church sat there and stared at him.

When he wanted to know why they weren't excited that he could suddenly read his text without glasses, his wife stood up and pointed to her eyes. That was when he realized the glasses he'd been looking for were on his face the whole time.

Then there was my friend who read his text and in a few moments was preaching about "blind Zacchaeus." Old blind Zacchaeus was begging by the road and old blind Zaccheaus.... He went on and on about poor old blind Zacchaeus. His wife finally stood up and interrupted him, to the smiles of the congregation, and reminded him, "It's blind Bartimaeus, not blind Zaccheaus."

I can see a few super-spiritual people in the church wondering what Bible school he attended. Church attendees might be overly quiet and spiritually cold where you attend, but Paul wrote that, "the "Kingdom of God is not eating and drinking; but righteousness and peace and joy in the Holy Spirit" (Rom. 14:17).

A close minister friend who is now retired was preaching in a large church and saw a woman sitting in the back row. He suddenly felt that he should pray for her. He stopped preaching and said, "Sister on the back row....yes you...the Lord told me that you are about to be delivered from a great burden." He asked her to stand up, only to discover she was pregnant and soon to give birth. The people laughed, the minister prayed for her, and the baby was born shortly thereafter.

DID THE DISCIPLES EVER LAUGH?

Ministry is always serious, as we deal with the eternal destination of men and women. However, when the people get together and fellowship— which is a code word for, "I'm hungry, let's go eat"—then conversations can turn humorous. Have you ever wondered what the disciples really thought after certain things happened? I'm not speaking from the spiritual standpoint, because after all, these were a group of common people who were men before they became men of God. Using my sanctified imagination, I can hear possible comments from a few:

"These all day crusades are wearing me out! I need a vacation!"

"He preached so long my bladder was about to burst."

"We have 5,000 men, not counting women and children. Where will they all go to the restroom?"

"Man, can you believe how bad Lazarus stunk? I thought I would throw up."

"Peter, your walking on water act is all washed up!"

"I'm falling asleep in these all night prayer meetings."

The reason I point this out is because of the comments I have heard

Christians make over the years. Some complained about visitors sitting in their special seat they had sat in for years, and proof that it belonged to them was the bronze nameplate on the armrest with their family's name on it! Then there were those who complained about the large crowds that had to park on the grass, and how the cars were killing the grass outside the church. One person suggested shutting down a revival because of the amount of toilet paper that people were using. An elder even complained that the young people were holding hands on the back row during a revival, which meant the revival had gotten out of order and should be shut down. I later learned that it was his granddaughter, and she was dating a boy he didn't approve of. So the solution, in his opinion, was to break them up by closing down a revival where 150 people had been converted.

For the more serious Believer reading this book, Solomon said, "There is a time to laugh" (Eccl. 3:4). Abraham's covenant son was named Isaac. In Hebrew, Isaac is Yitzak and means, "laughter." He was so named because he brought joy to his dad and mom in their old age—mom Sarah being ninety and Abraham being one hundred. Being a hundred years old and holding this infant and thinking, "I helped create this child!" would be enough to make any one-hundred-year-old man laugh!

CHURCH BLOOPERS

Mistakes not only occur in the secular world, but they can occur in a church setting, too. Below are church bloopers (mistakes) that appeared in church bulletins. Some are spelling mistakes that changed the entire meaning of the sentence, while others were incorrect sentence structure and grammar.

"Potluck supper Sunday at 5:00 pm. Prayer and medication to follow."

"Weight Watchers will meet at 7 pm. Please use the large double doors at the side entrance."

"Don't let worry kill you. Let the church help."

"Remember in prayer the men who are sick of our church and community."

"Please place your donation in the envelope along with the deceased person you want remembered."

"Low self-esteem group will meet Thursday at 7. Please enter through the back door."

"The pastor will preach his farewell sermon. Afterward the choir will sing, Break Forth with Joy."

"For those of you who have children and don't know it, we have a nursery downstairs."

"Thursday there will be a meeting of the Little Mothers' Club. All wishing to become little mothers, meet the pastor in his office."

I plead guilty to, purely by accident, having made my own bloopers from the pulpit. At times I will be talking so fast that I get my words turned around. Someone once asked, "If you are so anointed, then how do you get your words mixed up?" To that I answer, "The fire in my spirit is burning faster than my mouth can keep up."

CHILDREN WILL LAUGH AND THEN WANT A RERUN

One of the delightful attributes of children is that they love to laugh. And then they want a rerun. When my daughter was small, I would lift her with both hands and bounce her up and down. She would squeal with delight and say, "Do it again daddy, do it again." This continued until I finally had to say, "Okay, I'm done!"

For children, fun is contagious and repetitious. Just ask the child who comes into the living room when the relatives are visiting and does one thing that causes the group to laugh. They will repeat the act over and over until the laugher turns to smiles, and continue until people are no longer paying attention. Then they will discover another way of the doing the same thing. If you don't pay attention, you will hear, "Look at me! Watch me!" Eventually they return to their play routine and the adults move on to their next conversation.

Children love to laugh, and some want to be the life of the party. When I was around nine to twelve years of age, I wanted to be a comedian. Back in the days of Red Skelton, Hee Haw, and Carol Burnett, clean comedy acts were among the top viewed programs. But none seized my attention like the famous black comedian, Flip Wilson. Flip crossed racial lines and was very funny. Many of his comedy routines had religious themes, and one role was as pastor of The Church of What's Happening

Now. One skit was of a preacher's wife who returned from shopping for a new dress, and he titled it, "the devil made me buy this dress." I owned Flip's record album and memorized all of his skits. Whenever we had company in our home, I would offer to put on a comedy show, where I would recall from memory all of the skits on the album. I even parroted Flip's own lingo. There I was, a future stand-up comic, seeding his fame with an audience of a handful of people, getting laughs by repeating another comedian's work.

LEARNING TO LAUGH AGAIN

When George W. Bush was president, the media was quick to point out the gaffes he made. Some were really quite funny. A man who is President of the United States is not perfect, although many of his pundits prefer that he act as though he is. Gaffes are normal, and the world notices them when somebody's life is spent in the public eye and in front of the camera. One significant characteristic of President Bush was that he laughed at himself and poked fun at his own mistakes. This confused the liberal media, who didn't understand how he could lower himself to laugh about himself.

Recall the vehement criticism when Vice-President Dan Quale was asked to spell the word potato. Reading from the teacher's flash card that was being held up, he spelled the word with an "e" on the end, thus allowing his delighted critics to label him as totally incompetent. In a subsequent survey, the majority of Americans spelled it the same way. So while the secular media was making a mountain out of an e, the average American was saying, "What's the big deal?"

When we become so serious that we can no longer laugh, then we are refusing the medicine mentioned in Proverbs that creates a merry heart. Just as with my granddad, who was still joking and laughing as he was being wheeled into surgery at age eighty-four, there are two types of older people: those who are happy and those who are not. The Proverbs may help us understand why. We read:

"My son, do not forget my law,
But let your heart keep my commands;
For length of days and long life

And peace they will add to you."
"Trust in the Lord with all your heart,
And lean not on your own understanding;
In all your ways acknowledge Him,
And He shall direct your paths."
"Do not be wise in your own eyes;
Fear the Lord and depart from evil.
It will be health to your flesh,
And strength to your bones."
— Prov. 3:1-2; 5-8 (NKJV)

"The light of the eyes rejoices the heart,
And a good report makes the bones healthy."
— Prov. 15:30 (NKJV)

"A merry heart does good, like medicine,
But a broken spirit dries the bones."
— Prov. 17:22 (NKJV)

"A sound heart is life to the body,
But envy is rottenness to the bones."
— Prov. 14:30 (NKJV)

Your inward conflict and outward attitude affect not only those around you, but the life of God that is within you. The Word of God can penetrate to the soul and spirit, and the joints and bone marrow (Heb. 4:12). Negative actions that are contrary to the Word of God will draw the life-sustaining strength and joy from your mind, spirit, and eventually the very bones in your body.

When David sinned with Bathsheba, set up her husband to be killed, and covered his sin, he was exposed months later. He repented, but the lingering effect of his transgression was felt within his body. He wrote:

"Have mercy upon me, O Lord; for I am weak: O Lord, heal me; for my bones are troubled."

—Psalm 6:2

"For my life is spent with grief, and my years with sighing; my strength fails because of my iniquity, and my bones waste away."

— Psalm 31:10

Notice this verse; *"There is no soundness in my flesh because of your anger; neither is there any health in my bones because of my sin"* (Ps. 38:3). Unrepentant sin and sins linked with others will eventually affect your spirit, mind, and body—as proven by David, when the misery of his transgression began grieving his own soul.

However, he cried out to God, *"Make me hear joy and gladness; that the bones You have broken may rejoice"* (Ps. 51:8). David's desire was to have the strength to *rejoice*—a Hebrew word *giyl,* meaning not just to be happy, but to dance, spin around, and physically participate in an outward movement resulting from an inward feeling. David was a worshipper. Prior to his sin, he brought the Ark of the Covenant to Jerusalem where he danced before the Lord with all his might (2 Sam. 6:14).

David discovered there are two types of people in a worship service: the *participators* and the *observers.* Some *watch* while others *worship.* David danced in the streets while his wife watched from a window. She considered emotional expression in praising God to be on a lower level, as she was a queen and considered herself above all of that noise and emotionalism.

> *"Now as the ark of the Lord came into the City of David, Michal, Saul's daughter, looked through a window and saw King David leaping and whirling before the Lord; and she despised him in her heart."*
>
> *—2 Sam. 6:16 (NKJV)*

Critics of expressive worship look with condescension upon the true worshipers (John 4:23). They must not lower themselves and display emotion in the church. The fact is, all those folks sitting high up (in the window like Michal) and looking down on others are missing out on the joy, the fun, the fellowship, and the favor of God that is upon all of those people at street level who are spinning around, hand clapping, and arm waving.

Let me point out that the Ark of the Covenant, which carried the presence of God, was not resting peaceably in the upper chamber window of the palace with the critic who despised worship (2 Sam. 6:16). It was on the street where the celebration was in full swing—where children gathered with adults who were singing, spinning, and celebrating the Divine presence. God was no longer enclosed behind a curtain in a tabernacle; now He was on the streets where the common people lived.

To an atheist or agnostic, our verbal expressions and physical movements in worship are criticized as overly-emotional religious zeal. We are said to be making useless noise and worshipping an imaginary being that no one can prove exists. With that thought, consider a snowman. It's simply snow constructed to look like a round, jolly person. Children cannot hear him because he can't speak, nor can he touch them. He cannot run with him, and in fact he can't even walk. Yet the simplicity of being a child in the snow releases them from all limitations and inhibitions as they spin and dance, like David did around the Ark, because it is in the nature of a child to *make* and to *believe*.

So how can we dance to a God we cannot see? Because we are His creation, and part of our inner being, hidden in our DNA, knows that He is out there at the edge of the universe watching us. It was He who formed Adam from the dust of the ground, giving him his eyes, nose and mouth, and breathing life into a piece of clay and watching it come alive. As a child dances before his lifeless snowy creation, just as though it were a living being, so we who were not living beings were made. And we respond back to an invisible world because we believe.

LEARN TO REJOICE, NOT REJECT

David practiced *rejoicing,* and his wife practiced *rejecting.* It is sad to confess this, but some of the most critical and cantankerous people in North America are people who claim to be Christians. I have seen this in action on social media such as Facebook. A couple of years ago, I was preaching in Maryland. After the ladies cooked a seafood dinner for me and the team, I saw a large box of steamed crabs. I told Tiffany James, the daughter of my travel manager Robbie James, to take a picture of the crabs and post it on Facebook with the caption, "Perry enjoying kosher crabs."

Now, everybody knows that there is no such thing as kosher crabs. I wrote a book a few years ago called *Breaking the Jewish Code* and explained how that devout Jews and most Messianic Believers eat only kosher foods, which are based upon dietary laws in the Torah. So I knew that crabs are not kosher, and everybody who knows me knows that I know crabs are not kosher.

Tiffany monitored the response, and it didn't take long to find out how many people in the body of Christ cannot take a joke. Within an hour, twenty-seven-thousand people had viewed the picture. Some laughed, seeing the comedy and irony. Others commented that they love seafood. But there were plenty who made statements such as, "You have offended God! May He judge you for it!" Or, "You are an idiot! Crabs are not kosher!" One said that I insulted all the Jews in the world.

I waited until a few hundred comments had been posted. Then I posted back a response, saying this was a test to see the various reactions from Christians. Many had made certain *assumptions* that were not in the picture or the statement. Others judged by their *own opinions*. I quoted numerous Scriptures about food from the New Testament, and afterwards, did receive apologies from some for their mean-spiritedness.

Using another example, Pam received a message on her page from a woman who did not believe in celebrating any holiday throughout the year. She would not use the name of Jesus in prayer. She was one of the most negative people we had ever heard from, and she spoke as if nearly *all* Christians were deceived, and only a tiny handful carried the real truth. She later commented that none of her family liked her or wanted to be around her. After reading her negative and judgmental comments, Pam and I could understand why her family saw no benefit from being in her presence. Nobody wants to be around people who look with contempt upon everything others say or do. She had read so many different opinions on everything that even she was confused and had no joy in her system of beliefs.

As a Believer in Christ, the moment your beliefs begin to remove the peace and joy from your spirit, you have entered into *legalism* and not *righteousness*. The Kingdom of God is righteousness, peace, and joy in the Holy Spirit" (Rom. 14:17). Growing up in a Full Gospel denomination, the majority of our ministers were sincere in their commitment and solid in their doctrinal beliefs. However, they came across many times as mean-spirited and judgmental in their preaching, to the point that visitors and children of the members would leave the church and never return. Years ago, one man I knew summed up this attitude when he made this statement, "If I run all of them off, except me and my family, then so be it!"

It is easier to attract people with honey than vinegar, and easier to win a sinner through love than condemnation. It takes more muscles to frown than to smile. Unwise brains with big mouths are often negative, but controlled mouths with wise brains are trained to be positive and uplifting, and their words will edify others.

My grandmother once told me how that, in the 1930s, she saw a very strict minister discipline his son. He preached that any type of sports activity was evil, and when his son was caught playing basketball, he took a large leather razor strap and whipped the young man. These acts of discipline caused the son to turn from the church when he became eighteen, never to return. I asked my grandmother, "What good did all of that discipline do, if the son turned from God and never returned?"

Your peace in Christ will impress those tormented by sin as they seek what you have. Joy will attract them; bitterness will not. And laughter will break the ice in a cold room.

Redemption is serious business; in fact, it is a matter of life and death. Preaching must be firm but loving, strong but caring, disciplined but compassionate. I suggest that we learn to *mature in our spirituality* and at times *laugh at our humanity*. Since the Kingdom of God is peace, then relax more. Since it is joy, then smile more. Since it is righteousness, then enjoy your position in Christ and share it with others more.

Take this lesson to heart. Have fun in life, calm down, and relax. Life is too short. If you don't know how to have fun, watch a child. Anyone who can have fun dancing around a snowman can have fun doing just about anything.

CHAPTER 7

CHILDREN KNOW HOW TO SAY I'M SORRY

Three words—just three simple words—have at times saved a marriage, prevented a person from wallowing in pain, and kept relationships from being severed. Those three words are, "I am sorry." The two words that usually follow are, "Forgive me." The last three words that could pull you out of a marital doghouse are, "I love you."

As long as those words are sincere and heartfelt, they can prevent a divided relationship. But for some reason—pride, no doubt—our tongues become glued to the roof our mouth and we almost choke trying to say them when we ought to. Those words are a great three-step plan to preserving the people and relationships you love.

When a child has been caught doing something he shouldn't have done and is asked to apologize to a friend he hurt, after a couple of "It wasn't my fault!" excuses (wonder which parent they learned that from?), they usually say, "I'm sorry." Within a few minutes they are playing again and tearing into the toys like woman in a shoe store when everything's half off. If children have strong Christian parents, they usually understand that there are rewards for obedience and punishments for disobedience. They know that if they will humble their little spirit and apologize, things will go smoothly for them the rest of the day.

Somewhere between the *playroom* and the *workroom*, children grow up. As adults, we forget that simply saying, "I'm sorry" can have tremendous benefit for us, while refusing to admit any error could cost us in the future. I have known of individuals who had a falling out with someone over an issue that was a molehill turned into a mountain. They refused to see that their sour attitude was a hindrance to sweetening the problem, and they even began pointing fingers to place blame on everyone around them.

My wife and I personally know individuals who refuse to even speak to people or apologize in any manner for being the source of a major division or conflict. There is only one reason a person will never say, "I am sorry," and that is because of *pride.* In the King James translation of the Bible, the Hebrew word for pride is translated as, "haughtiness, highness, and swelling." Old timers would see a proud person and say, "They have a big head," which is a metaphor that means, their head is swelling because of their ego.

In 1 Timothy 3:6, the word *pride* (lest being puffed up with pride he fall into the same condemnation as the devil) is a Greek word meaning, "to envelop in smoke," and it means to be high-minded or to think more highly of yourself than you should. When a person is always bragging on themselves, we say they are "blowing smoke."

In ages past, pride is believed to be the original sin of Satan when he was expelled from heaven (Ezek. 28:17). There will be multitudes of people who will spend eternity separated from the Kingdom of God because they refused to humble their spirits and repent of their pride.

Several years ago a friend came to my office and told me about his dad's death. Without detailing his dad's past, he said that his father was a very hardened man who held a lot of grudges. Concerned for his eternal destiny, the son implored his dad to repent and forgive all the people he had wronged and those who had wronged him. Even while the angel of death was galloping toward his front door, this stubborn man refused to forgive anybody. He had lived too long, seen too much, and his mind was made up. Regrettably, as his son believes, he now has an eternity of remorse to regret those final minutes on earth when he refused to forgive and repent of his sins.

WHO DID IT?

When children are caught in an act of disobedience, especially when it involves another person, the blame game begins. "He hit me first… no, you hit me…I did not….yes you did!" Or we hear, "She took my doll…no I didn't, I was playing with it first." And of course, "It was your fault…no, it was yours." Usually at this point, mothers begin their ministry of intercession and reconciliation.

All mothers with children should have a common middle name—referee. At the birth of a child, all mothers should receive a gold-plated whistle and a book with referee hand symbols like time out, delay of game, and personal foul, along with a list of rewards and penalties for obedience and disobedience.

In order to stop two trains before they collide head-on, both must come to a halt before the final impact. The same is true when two children are arguing and the guilty party refuses to accept guilt and will not say, "I'm sorry." Both need to apologize to each other at the same time, and told to stop blaming someone else.

A man who shadowboxes, pretending he is in the ring with an invisible opponent, never gets knocked out but also never injures the shadow man. A person can be *disappointed* in themselves, but a person doesn't generally get *offended* at themselves. If they fail, they don't stare in the mirror and yell at their reflection, "You offended me! Why did you do that?" It takes two to box, two to wrestle, and two to fight. It also takes two to forgive and release each other from conflict to peace.

It would be easy to forgive others and say I'm sorry if an offended person was not so caught up in proving themselves right and the other person wrong. So what if you were right and they were wrong? What good have you done by turning a friend into an enemy, or a family member away from your fellowship? Some things are not worth the fight, and most petty differences top the list of things not worth fighting over. Saving your family, your church, and the souls of people are worth the battle; but childish conflicts are for childish thinkers, not mature adults.

Just as a child is taught the rewards and punishments for obeying or resisting instruction, we as Believers must go back to Scripture and understand that unforgiveness is the fruit of *not* saying I'm sorry.

Unforgiveness paves a path that leads down a dead end road called lost spiritual blessings. Unforgiveness also opens the door to mental and emotional torment (Matt. 18:21-35). Unforgiveness will hinder your prayers from being answered and even block your own forgiveness from God (Matt. 6:12-15).

RELIEF BY CONFESSION

Confession of an error or confession of sin brings immediate relief to a repentant person. Sin, strife, and unforgiveness are like lead weights, pressing upon the mind and spirit of the individual as they retain the tension created by unforgiveness.

Consider children, and watch their response after they have confessed that they are sorry. Within minutes, they are playing again as though nothing happened. It takes them becoming an adult before they discover that it's possible to hold a grudge for years or decades. Relief through confession is instant, and the burdensome weight you carry can fall off instantly.

Year ago, I heard a story of a couple who had a vehement argument before going to bed. That night the man died of a heart attack and the wife lived for years, regretting that her last words were a disagreement and not, "I love you." Before our marriage, Pam and I made an agreement that we would never go to bed angry with one another, and the last thing we would say before closing our eyes would be, "I love you." We chose this nightly routine so that, if one of us would pass away in the night, our last memory would be the expression of love toward one another. We have maintained this pattern since we married over thirty years ago.

It is easy for a child to be obedient when instructed to tell someone they are sorry. Is it easy for you?

CHAPTER 8

CHILDREN CRY AND DO SO IN PUBLIC

When my father was growing up in the mountains of West Virginia in the 1930s and 40s, the coal mines were booming. Every son grew up thinking he would follow the footsteps of his father into the black caverns deep under the mountains, and spend his life cutting chunks of black rock that helped keep electricity flowing and fires burning throughout America in the winter. This rugged and physically strenuous job often turned a potentially tenderhearted man into a calloused, cussing "old goat" who expressed his anger both verbally and physically as proof of his manhood.

Dad said that in his day, coal miners made it clear to their sons that real men don't cry.

This was so bred into the minds of the sons, that if a bully picked a fight and beat you up, you couldn't be a sissy and cry about it. If you were in a mining accident and broke a bone, it was okay to yell; but whatever you do, don't cry. Even at funerals of family and friends, the men could let the women folk cry, but the men were expected to act like men, because death comes to everybody.

This tough attitude carried over in the way the sons raised their own children, including the way they disciplined them, which was violent, at times. Often they were beaten with a thick leather miner's strap. Those under the wrath of the leather strap remember the pain that was, at times, unbearable. But if you were the victim, you were told to "take your medicine"'

One man expressed to me something he never forgot, even at the age of seventy. He said, "In those days, children never heard their dad tell them he loved them. That was the mother's responsibility. Maybe they didn't know how to express it, or maybe they thought it wasn't manly to say it. They didn't know how to properly discipline their children, either. The least agitation could cause a dad to suddenly slap the child across the face or pull off his belt and whip them until he beat bloody stripes on their body." This man confessed that, one day, he was kicked by his father so many times on his backside that he bled from the bowels that evening.

So in this culture, a generation was raised that was disciplined not to express any emotion. And that especially included weeping in a public setting. Yet, it was the wise King Solomon who wrote that there is a time to weep (Eccl. 3:4).

Years ago in Israel, I spoke to a survivor of the holocaust, the terrible tragedy where six million Jews perished under the Nazis. The years spent in the death camp, seeing Jews being shot, tortured, gassed, and burnt in ovens for no reason except that they were Jewish, was so traumatic that this Jewish man who survived the camp as a youth said, "I lost all emotion. Nothing moved me and I didn't want to feel anymore. I was emotionless and chose to be, because I never, ever wanted to cry again." Then he commented, "I was in Jerusalem when we recaptured the city in 1967 and I ran to the Western Wall where tens of thousands of Jews were dancing, singing, praying, and blowing shofars. I cried again for the first time in thirty-three years. This time it was for joy, because this is what my departed ancestors dreamed and spoke of before being murdered—the day that Jerusalem and Israel would become the permanent homeland of the Jews. And I had lived to see it."

There comes a time when it is okay for even grown men to cry. Just ask Jesus. If there was ever a masculine man, it was the Son of God, Jesus Christ.

JESUS WEPT

It is the shortest verse in the English Bible and it is only two words: *Jesus wept* (John 11:35). Jesus was sent to pray for his friend Lazarus, but He delayed His coming, allowing His friend to die. When He arrived in Bethany, the funeral was over and the corpse was in a limestone tomb, sealed by a large stone. The two sisters of Lazarus were interrogating Jesus, asking why He delayed coming for so long, because if He had come sooner, surely Lazarus would not have died.

As Jesus was standing at the grave, preparing to raise the corpse back to life, He wept. The question has been raised, "Why was He crying if He knew that He was preparing to bring His friend back from the dead?"

Most scholars indicate that Jesus felt grieved that His closest disciples did not comprehend the power given Him over death, and He wept because of their unbelief, just as He cried over Jerusalem for missing the time of their visitation (Luke 19:41-44).

If unbelief can cause Jesus to weep, then maybe that's why it rains buckets of water on earth, as heaven must be grieving with sadness at the sin, corruption, and unbelief that is destroying mankind. The sins in Noah's day were so terrible that it rained for forty days and nights (Gen. 7:4).

Anyone who has read the four Gospels would not doubt that Jesus was a physically, mentally, emotionally, and spiritually strong man. Any person who could survive the Roman flogging He received and still live to be crucified to death was not a weakling. His ability to resist the opposition that surrounded Him and put Satan in his place during the temptation demonstrates self-control and discipline (Matt. 4:3-11). I've been to Galilee and seen the area where He would have walked up and down those mountains to pray, and I can assure you that those mountains wear me out just looking at them. Yet, *Jesus wept.*

THE PERCEPTION OF HARDNESS

In England, protocol states that leaders should never express any form of emotion in public. The British perceive crying in public as a form of weakness. Even when Princess Diana was tragically killed, her two sons and her ex-husband never, that I recall seeing on television, shed a tear in public. They were required to put on a serious mask and hide any feelings of grief. After all, as military leaders are taught, the troops should never see you sweat, so never show weakness if you are a man. The public expects to see someone who is tough and hardened, so that nothing penetrates your emotions and makes you appear unstable or weak.

Yet, Jesus wept. Jesus threw out money changers and overturned tables in anger. Jesus rebuked religious leaders for their double standard, calling them snakes and hypocrites to their faces (Matt. 12:34). Those are rather emotional responses; yet intellectually, nobody was able to challenge His wisdom.

This may be one of the greatest hindrances in the church, politics, and society in general. We have either forgotten how to feel the pain of others, or we have become hardened and shut off that tiny water pipe that connects our emotions to our eyes. When a politician wept in public during his speech, overwhelmed with joy that he began with a simple life and now holds the position he does today, the liberal commentators thought the poor fellow had suddenly had a nervous breakdown. Could this be why so little gets accomplished in Washington D.C.? The politicians are hardened and tough, when they should be humble and broken over a nation in the condition that America is in today.

We as adults do this to our own children. As an infant, a mother will hurry to the crib, pick up her little darling, and hold her in her comforting arms until the crying ceases. We wonder, "Is she hungry, hurting, or needing a diaper change?" At age four, the same child falls down and bruises her leg. We pick her up and check out the scratches. We reach for a wash cloth, cover the scrape with antiseptic and a Band-Aid, and kiss it to make it feel better.

The child, at age ten, comes in the house crying because someone stole the bike from the yard. Now you are a counselor and a detective, giving advice and searching for the culprit, while reminding the child to stop crying; it's just a bike.

Five years later, the same daughter is in her room crying and wailing. You discover that the boy she has a crush on has broken her heart. "Quit crying," you halfway console her. "There'll be other boys and you need to grow up."

Thus the seed is planted. If you're really mature and grown up, you won't cry.

Life goes on. She turns twenty and someone hits her car. No big deal, just a fender bender. The unexpected accident frightens her and you receive a phone call. Overtop of the sniffling and shaking voice you comment, "Everything is okay. There's nothing to cry about as long as you're not injured. It can be fixed."

Notice that we allow an infant to cry. But by the time we are out of the pre-teen stage, we refuse to cry, especially in public, as emotion is misread as a sign of weakness or inability to cope with stress. Only with the death of a loved one does society permit you to cry. Lazarus was Christ's close friend, and Jesus wept.

GOD MADE TEARS

God gave us tears for more than protecting the eyes. In fact, there is a record in heaven of the number of tears you have cried, and they are even stored in a bottle and a book (Ps. 56:8). For some people, these bottles are empty; but for others, they are filled—perhaps the book records heart-breaking events that impacted your life, or prayers you have prayed during broken seasons of life. God promised us that, weeping may endure for the night, but joy comes in the morning (Ps. 30:5).

When Mary broke an expensive alabaster box, poured the precious ointment on Christ's head, and kissed and washed His feet with her hair and her tears (Luke 7:37-38), Christ considered it worship. Remember, worship means to "kiss toward or bow in homage to," and this woman was doing both (Luke 7:44-45).

In the story, it was two days before Passover (Matt. 26:2), and each year on the 14th of Nissan, Jews host the Passover Seder in their homes. Strict routines and precise rituals are maintained throughout the ceremony, with certain prayers and a story that never changes. Jesus was in Bethany in the house of a former leper named Simon during this time (Matt. 26:6). The meal and routine preparations of the feast were interrupted by a weeping woman. Her perfume with which she anointed Christ, her tears, and her kisses to his feet built a memorial for her, as to this day, we preach about her (Matt. 26:13). She was a sinner who was forgiven, and she expressed her appreciation by giving up something of *value* for something that was *priceless*—eternal life. The Pharisees couldn't appreciate her sacrifice as they were too self-righteous and unwilling to let go and let their hair down.

Who appreciates a healing more than others? A dying person who is raised up. Who appreciates freedom more than others? The person who was a prisoner and now is free. Who appreciates food? The person who was starving and now has food to eat. Who most appreciates a home? The person who was homeless and now has a warm bed.

Who *really* appreciates forgiveness from Jesus the most? From my own experience, it is the sinner who has been forgiven of much. Jesus said about this woman, *"Her sins, which are many, are forgiven, for she loved much. But to whom little is forgiven, the same loves little"* (Luke 7:47 NKJV). Crying comes easier for a person whose heart is sensitive with the love of God.

Tears are water, but they contain salt. In the early 1990s, I was considering this from a spiritual standpoint. Why would God have created tears and made them salty? In the Bible, salt was used as a preservative, but it would also be mixed with water and used to treat an infection or a shallow wound. Salt placed on a cut burns like fire. The spiritual application is that we generally cry in response to troubling news—an accident, a death, a divorce, or even fear. Certain circumstances can create a wound in our spirit that, if left untreated, will fester and spread, thereby affecting our spiritual condition and emotional state of mind. When we cry, we can taste the bitterness of the moment; but the salt reminds us that the infection and wound are only temporary and will be healed, as weeping is only for a season, and joy will come in the morning.

Instead of crying and allowing God to bottle our tears, we bottle up our feelings to prevent tears from flowing. If a person has ever been wounded by words, it is common to build up an internal resistance that prevents those feelings from coming to the surface again. This is one reason so many people become addicted to drugs and alcohol—to hide the pain and cover the hurts, so that the hurt will not override their emotions. Counselors say they are medicating themselves from emotional pain. Yet, it has been proven that there is healing in tears. Not in the tear itself, but in the fact that crying opens a person's inner spirit and allows it to become sensitive to receive ministry, counseling, and compassion from others.

Children cry easier, and sometimes for a foolish reason. They use crocodile tears to create drama, get what they want, and draw attention. Adults should never use tears to manipulate others under false pretenses. However, adults need to know that tears are a language that God understands, and they are given to us for a purpose. I have learned that you sure do feel better after a good cry. Just as a shower will cleanse your body, tears can purify your soul.

Weeping is a sign of humility, brokenness and sorrow; yet at other times, it signifies great happiness. It is not a sign of weakness when a man's heart becomes tender and he is moved to tears. No greater man has ever lived than Jesus, and Jesus wept.

CHAPTER 9

CHILDREN ADMIT
WHEN THEY
ARE HURTING

A funny incident once occurred between my wife Pam and me. If opposites attract, then we should be the spokespersons for Opposites Anonymous. There are no two people I know of whose personalities are so opposite, yet whose relationship compliments each other more. For example, Pam wants all the blinds in the house open and I want them closed. She loves windows and I prefer a room without them. She is continually pulled away by people who need attention, while I inform her to let the folks learn to do it themselves. She loves the sun, but I don't enjoy the heat. She relaxes at the pool, and I walk past it. She won't ride fast rides at the theme park, and I could be nicknamed king of the roller coasters. Pam is generally quiet and I am, at times, loud.

Despite our opposite traits, we are in love with each other and have wonderful times when we are together. That's because I have learned the secret of success: she is always right! (Just kidding. She's right only ninety-eight percent of the time.)

One time we had a heated disagreement and I was feeling badly about it. She was staring blankly out the passenger's window and saying nothing. I began to prod her with questions like, "What's wrong?" I thought that would be a good beginning. Her response was, "Nothing."

Then I said, "Come on, something's wrong. What is it?" She replied with the same rather dull comment, "Nothing." After a round of nothings, she saw my persistence and finally blurted out, "You've hurt me with what you said." I actually already knew that, but my male ego didn't want to initiate the first apology, as I was feeling a little hurt myself.

However, her statement didn't cause me to initiate a second round of a game of, who's right and who's wrong. But her words did release me to say how I regretted the disagreement, I was sorry, and I was madly in love with her. I have learned that a woman doesn't forgive and forget as easily or as quickly as a man does. A man will forget an argument with another man and go out to lunch half an hour later. Women will still be stewing about an argument years later.

The heart of the average child has not yet been tainted with *stains of unforgiveness* and entangled with *roots of bitterness*. They have not tapped into the art of *holding grudges*. Yet, in their little minds, their hurts are just as real as any grown-up hurts. Whoever said, "Sticks and stones may break my bones, but words will never hurt me," must have been hearing impaired. Words are like arrows that can cut to the spirit and even make the bones hurt (Ps. 64:3; 42:10).

Children are easily impacted by hurtful and careless words, including from other children. When I was in elementary school, I always felt compassion for any child required to wear glasses or even braces. I can remember the pain in their faces when some bully would yell, "Here comes four eyes," or "Hey, metal mouth."

My own life as a teenager, especially from ages thirteen to fifteen, was affected by the words of others. I was rather timid, didn't make a lot of friends, and wasn't involved in the party scene during any of my years in school. Seventh grade was like living out a horror movie. I was once singled out in an art class of thirty students, had my shoelaces tied together, told to hop around like a rabbit, and had my face shoved in paint, and demanded to lick paint off the floor. I was threatened to be beaten up if I refused. I went home afraid, telling my mom and dad, whose advice was, "It will be okay. Don't worry about it." I remember thinking, "You are not there, and you don't have to face these big bullies every day."

In reality, they didn't comprehend the seriousness of the fear that I was feeling, which began to affect my grades. The only people, I later discovered, who really understood me were the other kids in school who were being bullied by the same group. *It took someone with the same pain to understand my pain.*

HURTING BEHIND THE MASK

Masking the pain is a phrase used to describe the act of using different methods to hide behind hurts. Speaking of pain, in recent years my heart has been turned to the younger generation that is experiencing so much pain from abuse, divorce, broken relationship, and battles with oppression. The numbers of youth turning to alcohol and drugs is at an epidemic proportion. In my North American travels, I have met numerous young people who were addicted to alcohol or some form of illegal drug, such as cocaine, heroin or meth.

Voice of Evangelism supports a women's ministry called Women of Hope, and they assist addicted women of all ages, bringing them into a life of freedom through Christ. Many of these women have expressed that their own personal pain and rejection opened the doors to a demon of addiction. At the time they were unaware that they could cast their cares upon the Lord (1 Pet. 5:7), and unaware that the Lord could heal their broken heart and bind up their wounds (Ps. 147:3). The drugs were used to dull the pain, to help block out reality, and to escape into a fantasy land of nothingness that led to nowhere.

But the drugs only extended their road of misery and lead to depression and thoughts of suicide. They knew they were hurting, but felt there was nobody who understood their pain. They didn't know what could ease their suffering. Alcohol and drugs became the mask they hid behind, thinking they were avoiding their pain. But it returned when the mask was gone; and in fact, it made their problems worse.

Most children will never wear a mask when it comes to admitting how much they hurt. When you are comforting them after a fall, they will say, "But Mommy, it really hurts." As a caring and loving parent, how do you feel when you hear that tender voice, see those sincere tears, and hear that helpless whimper telling you it hurts? Isn't your reaction to stop what you are doing, pick them up in your arms, and find a solution to stop the pain? A caring parent will respond to the cry of their hurting child.

HOW THE HEAVENLY FATHER RESPONDS

The lack of loving and affectionate earthly fathers has kept people from understanding the traits of a loving heavenly Father. Earthly dads are often absent and living in a distant world of their own. One young woman told of her parents' divorce and how, as a young girl, she would lie in the bed and cry for her dad to come and tuck her in the bed. He never did.

But God becomes our heavenly Father and adopts us into His family the moment we enter a redemptive covenant through His Son. Our cries are like a magnet drawing God toward us. This truth can be seen when we examine the many Hebrew names of God that are found in the Old Testament—names that reveal God's character and nature and His love for His creation. One unique name for God was revealed to Abraham:

> *"When Abram was ninety-nine years old, the LORD appeared to Abram and said to him, 'I am Almighty God; walk before Me and be blameless.' "*
>
> *—Genesis 17:1 (NKJV)*

In Hebrew, *Almighty God* is two words, *El Shaddai*. The Hebrew word *El* means *a strong and mighty one*, and the word *Shaddai* is derived from a root word *shad,* which in the Semitic language refers to the breast of an animal that nourishes its young. In Hebrew the word is feminine, which also has a bearing on the uniqueness of this name. Hebrew teachers often say this name means that God is *the many breasted one*, referring to the fact that God nourishes His children. This image of God shows how He is similar to a nursing mother who responds to the cries of her child by feeding and nourishing the infant.

You have heard it said that a person can only receive help when they want it and ask for it. We often ignore our hurts because we think we can deal with them ourselves, or because we fear further hurt or rejection from others. Thus we seal our mouth and our heart. For some, the seal is caused by pride. They are too proud to admit they failed, too embarrassed to admit what occurred, or too fearful of drawing other people into their web of pain.

When Peter was walking on water, he stepped out in *faith* but began sinking with *doubt*. Just before his head bobbed under, he was heard yelling three significant words: "Lord save me!" (Matt. 14:30). With this quick prayer, Jesus reached out and pulled Peter out of a watery grave.

There are three words that can assist you and bring a divine reversal—the words, "Lord, it hurts." These words express that you are in pain and are turning to El Shaddai for enough strength to seize God's attention and move His healing hands in your direction, like a surgeon preparing to remove a dangerous growth from your body.

Peter was considered a rather outspoken apostle. But when you are soaking wet, treading water and ready to drown, it is no time to ask for a blow dryer and a change of clothes. It's time to yell HELP!

Children, in their tender simplicity, are never hesitant to tell you when they are hurting. They don't do this just because they want to tell you it hurts; they also do it because they know a parent will comfort them. The atoning work of Jesus was for the body, soul, and spirit—and includes the emotional well-being of those who believe upon Him.

A doctor is useless unless you are willing to *admit* and *submit*: admit that you are sick and submit to his care. Admit to the Great Physician that you have pain from the past, and submit to His authority and care for your future. Children will tell you when it hurts, because they know that someone will understand and fix it. If a child can do it, then why can't we?

Human nature can be quite complicated. We separate over political parties, but unite during a national disaster such as we experienced on September 11, 2001. We separate over religious or denominational affiliations, but unite at one church for a candlelight vigil after a child has been killed. We mind our own business when it comes to being involved with our neighbors, but we work tirelessly like ants to rebuild a home that has been hit by a storm.

People might reject your message, your style of ministry, or your methods; but it is virtually impossible to reject pure, unconditional love. The warmth from a loving heart can melt the ice of another's heart, just like the sound of, "I love you" from a child's lips will bring joy and a smile to the receiver. Everyone needs to hear and be impacted by the words, "I love you."

CHAPTER 10

CHILDREN LOVE TO HOLD HANDS AND KISS

Iwas born ON June 23 in a small rural town in West Virginia. Shortly after my birth, the doctor and my parents knew something was wrong, because I was unable to hold down milk. The doctor tried several different formulas and I could keep down none of them. They released my mother from the hospital and kept me for two weeks, trying to diagnose and resolve the problem. Eventually I was able to keep down whole milk.

My mother told me a few years ago that the hospital would not let her hold me for two weeks, and she had to view me through the glass nursery window. When she told me that I laughed and said, "Now that explains it."

"Explains what?" she asked.

I replied, "I just read where the most important part of an infant's life is the first few weeks of being held by the mother. Now I know why I love to hug my close friends, because nobody hugged me as a newborn."

She laughed and reminded me that I was hugged by her and still am. As of this writing, she is seventy-seven years of age.

All children, no matter where they live in the world, have a love and response trigger. They also shy away from angry, mean-spirited and temperamental individuals whose countenances express their negative emotions. I am a very affectionate person by nature. From the time I was a child, I would hold my mother's and grandmother's hands while seated beside them on a couch or near them in a car. I am uncertain if this nature is part of my personality, or my Italian blood (since most Italian families are very affectionate). From the time my children came into this world, I would hold them close and give them kisses.

We have a 1989 home video of our son after we brought him home from the hospital when he was born. At that time I sported a heavy mustache, and in the video I am dancing around the basement on New Year's night, kissing the little fellow under his chin and tickling him with the mustache. He is smiling and responding with a rather anemic giggle. By the time our daughter arrived in 2001, the mustache had become a goatee, and she received kisses under her chin, too. However, she would laugh with a loud chain of giggles that would brighten any parent's day.

If you haven't raised children, let me tell you that boys are different from girls. As boys mature, they tend to lean more toward Mom's advice and attention, while little girls tend to seek Dad's affection and approval. For years now, our daughter has heard me make a statement that I reminded her of when she was born and had no clue what I was saying to her. I told her that I would give her one million kisses before she would ever be married, and I would spoil her so that she would need to find a man like her daddy who would care for her and love her like her daddy does. So from time to time, my little princess will come through the house and I will change my voice slightly and announce to her with a long draw, "A millllllion kissssesss for Amanda Michele."

Since she has been able to speak, she has asked me how many kisses she has gotten from me. I told her that I lost count at about ten thousand, and I remind her that it will take some time for me to complete my kissing assignment.

I can still hear those silly infant giggles in my head from both of my precious children! Now that Amanda is older, she raises her eyebrows and tilts her head as if to say, "Dad, you are really crazy."

Most children crave affection and attention from both of their parents, but especially from a father. There are so many wounded hearts and bruised men and women who felt personal rejection when their biological father divorced their mother or walked out on them for whatever reason. I read many years ago that a child receives his understanding about God from observing his father's care. How does he act, and how does he treat people, especially the child? If this is true, then imagine the wrecked image of God that young people grow up with because of an absent or wicked father!

Before I proceed, let me say that God is far superior to any earthly father, as God is faithful never to leave nor forsake you (Heb. 13:5). He is filled with love for you.

POWER OF TOUCH

As children we loved to hold hands and get kisses from our parents. There has been some amazing research conducted regarding the healing power of touch. One report from the University of Virginia revealed that holding hands helps reduce stress. During the research, wives wore electrodes to measure what happened when holding their husbands' hands. They were told they would receive a mild shock, and the imagery showed the reaction of the area of the brain that handles threats. When holding their husbands hands and told it was coming, scans revealed the brain was much calmer with the husband's touch.

Research has also been done on kissing. The lips are densely packed with nerve endings. When you kiss, feel good chemicals are released in the brain and stress is reduced. A German study says that a man who kisses his wife before leaving for work lives an average of five years longer, takes fewer sick days, and earns twenty to thirty percent more income. Guys, that's a good reason to remind your wife to pucker up—so you can live to be an old man. Touching the hand and rubbing the back of a person's shoulders or even their feet increases hemoglobin in the body which, in turn, creates a relaxing feeling.

KISSING GOD

Have you ever heard of kissing God? Let me explain. The word worship is found in this form of the word 108 times in the English translation of the Bible. The common Old Testament word is *shachah,* which means "to prostrate oneself before; paying homage to a deity by bowing or falling down." It is first used in Genesis 22:5, where Abraham was leading his son Isaac to the top of Mount Moriah to offer him before God as an offering. Abraham placed Isaac on the altar before God in an act that he called worship.

The New Testament Greek word for worship, translated thirty-five times as the word *proskuneo,* means "to kiss toward." The imagery is of a dog that licks its master's hand, and can also refer to prostrating oneself before a greater one, paying respect or reverence. In the time of the Roman emperors, the word denoted bowing before the emperor as a deity and kissing his ring. Real worship involves becoming intimate with God, and intimacy requires closeness.

God loves to be "kissed" with the words of our mouth and praises from our lips, and this is one of the ways we worship Him. Worship brings Him closer to us, because when we draw near to God, He will draw near to us (James 4:8). There is a Jewish tradition that, when Moses died, God kissed him (called the kiss of death) to release his spirit from his body, and then God personally buried him (Deut. 34:5-6). A kiss is an expression of a close friendship or relationship.

Those who claim to love God should enjoy worshipping God. And if the praise for Him is in your heart, then it will come out of your mouth (Matt. 12:34). When we worship God in spirit and in truth (John 4:23), then His presence becomes tangible and can be felt. Believers often describe this feeling as warmth, joy, peace, or even electricity or energy. Just as a natural kiss releases "feel-good" chemicals, real worship releases a unique feeling from God's presence.

Those of us who have children love them dearly and enjoy expressing affection and showering them with attention. However, have you noticed what begins to occur the older they get? When they hit those teenage years, they certainly don't want to be seen in public holding their mom or dad's hand.

And they often remind their parents not to *ever* kiss or hug them in front of their friends! Soon their attention is drawn to the person they will eventually marry, and their love and affection is expanded from their parents to their own family. Dads, get ready. Your daughters will be attracted to another man one day.

I once heard someone say that they still had a *relationship* with God, but were out of *fellowship* with Him. The Greek word fellowship is *koinonia*, and means an intimate partnership (Phil. 1:5; 2:1; 3:10 etc.). A marriage has no *relationship* if there is no fellowship, intimate friendship, and partnership. Let any husband try to have an intimate relation*ship* with his wife without having intimate fellow*ship* and he will soon discover he is alone without any *ship*.

As a new babe in Christ, we were excited about our new-found faith. We anticipated going to church, we freely clapped and lifted our hands during the worship experience, and we verbally expressed our words of love to our Heavenly Father. Years passed and we became older and more mature. It is not that we have *forgotten* how to kiss (worship) God; it is that we have grown so accustomed to it, that it has little meaning anymore. We have seen it all, gotten it all, and don't need it anymore.

It reminds me of the New Testament family from Bethany—Mary, Martha and Lazarus—whose actions reveal a practical application in the church. We read where Mary was *worshipping* at Christ's feet, while her sister Martha *worked* in the kitchen, and Lazarus just *sat* at a table (John 12:2-3). In each church there are these three groups: worshipers, workers, and sitters. Guess which one died? Lazarus, the sitter.

These sitters, whom I call pew warmers, have ceased their intimate worship and now fold their arms with a bless-me-if-you-can attitude. In my observation, these are spiritually the deadest and driest members in any church. They often look at their watches and note the closest exit, so that the moment the last amen is spoken, they can run out to beat everybody else to the restaurant. They sit down *too long* and get up *too soon*, while the presence of the King of kings is hovering in the atmosphere. You can sit in one spot so long that you die (2 Kings 7:3). Solomon had a word for these folks about being in a king's presence. He wrote:

> *"Do not be hasty to go from his presence. Do not take your stand for an evil thing, for he does whatever pleases him. Where the word of a king is, there is power; and who may say to him, 'What are you doing?' "*
> *—Eccl. 8:3-4 (NKJV)*

Children, especially daughters, love their father's affection. But as their hearts turn toward a new man, their husband, they neither expect nor think it is necessary to receive the same level of attention from Dad. Now a new lifetime love has captured her heart. Dads understand this when his little girl becomes a woman, and the day comes when he stands beside his daughter in a black tuxedo and prepares to release her into a sacred covenant of marriage. Another man will hold her, love her, kiss her, and provide for her. On her wedding day, he realizes that Daddy's girl, whom he has protected from birth, has now become another man's woman.

Here is the spiritual application. When Believers begin to look for love or attention from a source outside of their Heavenly Father, their attention and affection can be turned away, and their hearts can become cold. This happened in the early church, which is why Christ rebuked the church at Ephesus, saying they had left their first love, and why He reprimanded the church at Laodicea for their lukewarm attitude (Rev. 2:4; 3:16). Ancient Israel was rebuked for playing the harlot with many lovers (Jer. 3:1). In nineteen verses of the Old Testament, Israel is rebuked for going after other lovers, as if God's attention and care were not enough to satisfy them.

WE HAVE FORGOTTEN HOW TO KISS

As a babe in Christ, all things are made new (2 Cor. 5:17). All truth is new, the messages are new, and the songs being sung are new. A new convert is like a child in a candy store; so many amazing messages, new friends, activities to choose from, and continual excitement. I have seen thousands of converts come to Jesus through my ministry and have always admired their simple faith and zeal. They cannot wait to leave work each day and prepare for that night's church service. Once the presence of the Heavenly Father has descended into the sanctuary, the new babes lose track of time and don't worry about getting home early. They enjoy holding hands with God and kissing Him with their words in worship. They sense His embrace and love. It is a little bit of heaven on earth.

During my early extended revivals, when the glorious presence of God was blanketing the atmosphere, I would say, "Heaven and earth have kissed, and we are caught in the middle of the smack!" That is my way to explain the atmosphere a Believer experiences through true worship. Real worship is our way of expressing our affection toward our heavenly Father.

When we mature in our relationship with Jesus, the danger is that we can become so familiar with our Heavenly Father that we eventually perfect the religious routine and form that replaces the presence. The rituals are so perfected in most churches that a fellow church member can be at home, look at the clock, and know the precise flow of the service because the routine never changes. They know there will be an opening prayer, two congregational songs, prayer requests, three more songs, a thirty-minute sermon, and a dismissal prayer. Some churches have this timed, right down to the very minute. And of course, we need good lighting, an efficient heating and air conditioning system, and great music.

Eventually other lovers—called the cares of life, deceitfulness of riches, and lust of other things—overtake our time and capture our attention. Our bodies are sitting on a pew, while our mind is somewhere else and telling us to hurry out as quickly as possible.

BEWARE OF FALSE LOVERS

We are all familiar with the story of King David. He was assigned to be a young shepherd who also was a man after God's own heart (1 Sam. 13:14). He singlehandedly slew bears and lions to protect his father's flocks, and eventually he killed a giant named Goliath who was tormenting the entire Hebrew army (1 Sam. 17:31-36). His fame and favor exalted him to a position of king of Judah, and then king of Israel.

David was undoubtedly loyal to God for many years, until one day a fine looking married women created more damage than a bear, a lion, or the entire Philistine army ever did. After committing adultery and getting the wife of Uriah pregnant, David had her husband slain in battle. This plunged his favorable ratings and brought a reproach against God's name. His own sons began to initiate rebellions in the kingdom, and his son who was conceived by Bathsheba died shortly after birth (2 Sam. chapters 11 and 12).

In his time of personal grief, condemnation and guilt, David could have reminded God of his years of faithfulness and asked God not to allow him to lose his prosperity or his kingdom, and to restore the respect and integrity he once had. He could have hired a marketing firm to meet with his staff and prepare a plan of action to defend the king's impeccable reputation by making the woman look guilty and calling it a seductive setup or an inside political hack job by David's enemies to ruin his reputation.

Instead David humbled himself. He sought God's forgiveness and mercy, and asked the Heavenly Father not to take His Spirit from him, and to restore to him the joy of salvation (Psalms 51:9-12). David lost his impeccable reputation forever, but he refused to forever lose God's presence.

DANCING WITH BROKEN BONES

In Psalm 51, which is identified with David repenting for his sin, he presents a powerful petition to God by requesting:

> *"Make me hear joy and gladness, that the bones You have broken may rejoice."*
>
> —*Psalms 51:8 (NKJV)*

Numerous Hebrew words in the Old Testament are translated as *rejoice* in the English Bible. The word that David used here is the Hebrew word *giyl*, and it does not mean to be happy again. Instead, it is derived from a Hebrew root word meaning, "to spin around with a violent emotion; often under extreme joy." David was a worshipper and a dancer (2 Sam. 6:14). David danced in the streets when the Ark of the Covenant was brought to Jerusalem to place in a temporary tent known to Hebrew scholars as the tabernacle of David (1 Chron. 15). David loved his intimacy with God, and he prepared a special team to minister continually before the Ark with singing, worship, and songs. Many of the songs found in the Psalms were recorded while worshipers ministered at David's tabernacle.

David's sin had given him a spiritual and emotional wound that affected his confidence—not in God, but in himself. His failure was known to everyone. Enemies that once feared his name now mocked him as a weakling, subject to failure. David knew he was a broken man; but his request to God was to once again allow him to dance and rejoice.

Perhaps you have been focused on the wrong things in your prayer. Are you seeking the blessing instead of the blesser? The gift instead of the giver? Prosperity instead of the presence? Personal satisfaction instead of peace? Perhaps you need to spend more intimate times with your Heavenly Father, reading His love letter to you (the Bible) and sending kisses to Him in worship and prayer. Little children love the attention of their mother and father, and children love to hold hands and kiss. Don't ever get so old that you forget how to kiss God.

CHAPTER 11

CHILDREN WANT TO HEAR AND SAY I LOVE YOU

When I see a dad with a newborn child, pride radiates from his face like the sun rising over a mountain, initiating the beginning of a new day. I tell that new father, "If you think you are enjoying yourself now, just wait until your precious little gift runs into your arms and says, 'Daddy, I love you!' " Children might not recall those times, but parents certainly do.

Many years ago I was conducting a revival, and my wife and I were staying in a small apartment in the family life center next to the church. I was having a difficult time emotionally and had slipped into the dark gymnasium where I sat in an old rocking chair and told the Lord that I needed to hear from Him. I asked Him not to send some adult who knew how I felt, just to give me comfort. I wanted an angel to appear with a message.

I kept sitting there in the dark, where the only light was reflecting from the brightly lit hallway that led to the room where we were staying. Ten, fifteen, and then twenty minutes passed. Suddenly the door opened and in marched my four-year-old son in his pajamas, running toward me with just enough light to see me in that rocking chair. He immediately jumped into my lap, touched my face with his hands and said, "Daddy, I love you very, very much," and then he fell asleep in my arms. I looked up with tears and thanked God for sending me an angel—a little one in a human body whose words touched my heart.

My daughter has often reminded me that she thinks I'm the best dad in the whole wide world. When she began saying that at a young age, I would always reply to her, "Your love is melting me like butter!" She would giggle and say, "I love you, Daddy." Hearing this from your children is the greatest present they could ever give you, and it is the greatest feeling in the world. My wife even occasionally gets in on the action and tells me what a great husband she thinks I am. But we'll save that for another day.

DO YOU REALLY LOVE ME?

The word love is used in the English translation of the Bible 310 times. However, there are different Greek words used to identify the different expressions of love found in human nature or in God's Kingdom. Jesus taught that we should love our neighbor as ourselves (Matt. 5:43). This word love is *agapao* and refers to much love.

We then read where the Pharisees loved to be seen in public places (Matt. 6:5; 23:6). The Greek word here for love is *phileo*, which is more of a brotherly form of love. It can also mean to be fond of someone or someplace, such as saying "I love living in Tennessee."

Peter had one of the worst weeks in his ministry career when he cut off a man's ear, denied that he knew Jesus, and saw the death of Christ. The Lord asked Peter three times, "Do you love me more than these?" (John 21:15). Previously Peter denied Him three times, but here he affirms his love for Christ three times.

Have you ever considered how difficult it is for any person to reject being truly loved? There are some who confuse a fleshly lust or passion for love, but this is a counterfeit emotion that keeps a person from experiencing the reality of true love. Many girls willingly give their bodies to a testosterone-controlled young man, and later confess that they just wanted to be loved by someone.

Paul told us the signs of real love when he wrote:

"Love suffers long and is kind; love does not envy; love does not parade itself, is not puffed up; does not behave rudely, does not seek its own, is not provoked, thinks no evil; does not rejoice in iniquity, but rejoices in the truth; bears all things, believes all things, hopes all things, endures all things. Love never fails."

—*1 Cor. 13:4-8 (NKJV)*

I am now over the age of fifty, and as I ask for more wisdom to work wiser instead of harder, the more understanding I become when dealing with people and their issues. I was recently asked, "What has been the greatest change in your personal beliefs since you began ministry?" I answered, "I believe there will be some people in heaven that I thought *wouldn't* make it, and some people that I thought *would* make it who might not be there." This is not necessarily a change in belief, but an observation. It is the truth revealed by Paul in 1 Corinthians 13, which is that love is really what matters.

Growing up in a strict, Full-Gospel church, we often felt a lot of condemnation after we heard a message about sin. At times we didn't feel perfect enough or holy enough to be accepted by the Lord. We felt like we were failing or falling short of the requirements the minister and the church placed upon us to be holy and sanctified Christians. If a carnal thought even crossed our minds, we immediately thought God hated us. We just knew we were on the road to being a backslidden prodigal son.

I was eighteen years of age when I went into a Christian bookstore and discovered a little thirty-two page booklet that explained the New Covenant. While this teaching was an age-old truth, the information in this booklet was still a great revelation for me. I realized that Jesus really does love me! In this redemptive covenant, *God loved me more than sin could defeat me.* This fact made me realize it was His grace flowing through His mercy, and not my works flowing through my body, that sustained me in His love.

Based on this personal revelation, I have made two statements for many years. First, God's love for us is greater than the devil's hatred of us. And second, God's ability to preserve us is greater than any attack Satan can bring against us. God's love is His hedge around us, His mercy in us, His favor with us, and His power upon us. He does everything that He does because He loves us. God loved us so much that He gave His only begotten Son, that whoever believes on Him will not perish but have everlasting life (John 3:16). He who does not love does not know God, for God is love (1 John 4:8).

If you feel a spark of energy in your heart when your children and grandchildren say, "I love you," then imagine the heart of the Heavenly Father when He hears you say, "Abba Father, I love you." Learn to love like a child does, without complicating things.

CHAPTER 12

CHILDREN ALLOWED JESUS TO TOUCH THEM

In Matthew 19:13-15 we read, *"Then little children were brought to Him that He might put His hands on them and pray, but the disciples rebuked them. But Jesus said, 'Let the little children come to Me, and do not forbid them; for of such is the kingdom of heaven.' And He laid His hands on them and departed from there."*

Have you ever pulled up to a fast food establishment and stepped inside to get lunch, when suddenly two vans from the local day care arrive, and here comes an army of miniature eating machines jumping up and down with their colorful backpacks that are almost as big as their own bodies? Before you can place your order, here comes a jolt of hyperactive energy in human form that sounds like a forest of chirping birds at the local zoo. You can't understand what any of them are saying, because they are yelling over top of each other as they attempt to inform their fearless leader what their bellies are yearning for. You wait, and wait, and wait, realizing that by now, you could have made it through the drive through three times.

Now travel back to the time of Christ when five thousand men, plus women and children (Matt. 14:21), filled the natural outdoor stadium on the hills in and around Galilee to hear life changing teaching from Jesus of Nazareth. They also came to receive prayer and to be healed of various illnesses and maladies. Suddenly, here came those pesky little children, some covered with dirt from playing on the hillside, some barefoot from playing in the grass, all running toward Jesus after His message was completed.

As these future church members and leaders gathered around the Messiah, I can picture some of the adults who had traveled a long distance to receive prayer moving toward the disciples and saying, "I have come many miles and His message was longer than usual. There are things I must get done back home, so if you wouldn't mind, could you please get those kids away from Jesus? They're holding up the prayer line."

Perhaps Peter instructed, "Clear a line. See all these sick folks here? Let's not waste precious time!"

The disciples moved toward Christ and rebuked the children. But instead, they received a rebuke from Christ, who told them to leave the children alone, for such is the kingdom of heaven (Matt. 19:14).

When Christ spoke, in the audience were many Sabbath-keeping, tithe-paying, feast-observing, law-abiding sons and daughters of Abraham. They had to wait in line while the children received their personal blessing.

> *"And they brought unto him also infants, that he would touch them: but when his disciples saw it, they rebuked them. But Jesus called them unto him, and said, Suffer little children to come unto me, and forbid them not: for of such is the kingdom of God."*
>
> —*Luke 18:15-16 (KJV)*

One thing is certain. Jesus must have been a friendly person, because children are hesitant to spend time with a frowning, gruff, stern-looking man whose countenance makes a person think they were baptized in lemon juice. Children tend to be drawn to happy people. Have you ever noticed that in most historical paintings of Christ, especially from the Renaissance period, the artist seldom made Him smile or look happy? He is always somber and serious, somewhat like a monk from a monastery who has lived as a recluse most of his life.

WHAT DID JESUS SAY?

When blessing infants, some picture Jesus as placing His right hand of authority on the heads of the children and saying, "I bless thee." Some believe that Christ surely spoke the old King's English, saying thee instead of you, for certainly this would have been required for it to be a proper blessing.

However, I picture Jesus carrying on a brief conversation with some of the older Jewish children, whose parents were in the crowd that afternoon. He might have said, "What did you think about that story I told?" Or, "Did you get to see the miracles God did today? Isn't it wonderful what God can do?" On a more personal note He may have asked, "Have you ever gone fishing in the Sea of Galilee?"

I believe the children were engulfed in the persona and ministry of Jesus. How can I say this? Having heard so much from their parents and others about Jesus, I am certain the children were in awe after being up close with Him.

We have a bit of experience with children and ministry, because having an international television ministry brings you into the homes of millions of people, and many have children in the home. After several years of watching a weekly program, these children grow up feeling like you are part of the family, although they have never met you. At times I will walk into the local Cracker Barrel restaurant and pass a little fellow, perhaps four to six years of age. Suddenly I will hear that high pitched voice from behind me announcing to his mother, "Mommy, that's Perry Stone. That's the man on TV." If possible I will speak to the mother or father, and then say hello to the child. I love to see the child's expression; I'm just a minister, but to them I'm a man on television. Often they just stare like a deer blinded by headlights and say nothing. It is delightful to see and hear these little ones. On one occasion, a little boy saw me and said, "Mommy, there's the Jesus man!" What an honor to be recognized by a child as the Jesus man.

If you don't think your child pays attention in church, think again. Parents often tell me how their son or daughter came home and told the other children what they heard in church, and all the time the parent thought they were entertaining themselves by sketching on a piece of paper. Many times those simple stick people on that paper are intended to be an angel standing behind the preacher, or Jesus standing beside the preacher, or a crooked and skinny preacher etched from a child's mind onto paper. The message becomes art and art becomes the message.

Occasionally, a little boy or girl will run up to me, hand me a piece of paper folded more times than a one dollar bill in a church offering, and skip away without saying a word. I will unfold the sheet and there will be a big heart with a Bible or a cross, with scribbled letters that read, "I love you Perry Stone." That is something that will bring tears to my eyes. And somehow, I believe that's how Jesus felt when He blessed the children who surrounded Him.

CHILDREN AREN'T AFRAID OF JESUS

It appears that no child was afraid to receive the touch of Jesus, or to have Him lay His hands upon their heads and bless them. But there are grown adults today who have no interest in Jesus touching them. A sudden jolt from the heavenly world or a quickening from the Holy Spirit could release tears and streak that pretty make up that you spent fifteen minutes applying.

Then there are those friends from work that you invited to the service. The last thing you need is a blessing from heaven that would cause your colleagues to view you as emotionally unstable or a religious fanatic.

Children have a simple childlike trust and are not inhibited by the same things that hinder Mom and Dad. Adults can become professional Christians and learn how to pretend, or as we sometimes say, "fake it until we make it." They put on a happy face when their heart is breaking. They speak that church lingo, calling each other brother and sister, while behind the scenes they treat that same church family with disrespect through gossip that they often veil with the excuse, "I am simply concerned."

Children, on the other hand, haven't learned to address the more academically inclined, highly educated minister as Doctor. They are more concerned about getting to church early to see their friends, while the parents are concerned about planning an early escape to be the first in the long line of traffic leaving the parking lot.

From children and their childlike faith, we can learn what faith really is. It simply means to believe and to trust. Some overly-educated Christians consider this definition too simplistic and irrational. To the intellectuals who must have something proven to them before they will believe it, God must be complicated, detailed, difficult to understand, and almost impossible to comprehend. Yet a child knows this one thing. God is big enough to rule the entire universe, but small enough to live in their heart. As we've heard it said, big things come in small packages. And a little faith can take you a long way on the road to believe.

CHAPTER 13

CHILDREN WANT
TO KEEP IT SIMPLE

You have probably heard the term, "just plain vanilla." Vanilla is a flavoring that is used in desserts, ice cream, and specialty coffees. We have all enjoyed vanilla ice cream or a vanilla milk shake. But when we use the term, "plain vanilla," we mean that something is *plain and simple*.

I have been a Christian for many years and I understand that new converts (babes in Christ) need spiritual milk, or the simplicity of the Word. Stronger and more mature Believers desire the meat of the Word (Heb. 5:12-13), or the deeper teaching that feeds their spirit and challenges the intellect. So we begin with the simplicity of vanilla ice cream. Then we can add bananas, scoops of chocolate and strawberry ice cream, chocolate syrup, whipped cream and cherries, and call it a banana split. For some, vanilla is just too plain and simple to enjoy by itself.

I will be the first to confess that I have bypassed the simplicity of just plain vanilla for the more complicated banana split. After studying the Bible for thirty-six years and researching for an untold number of sermons, books and articles, I find myself under pressure to dig deeper and study longer for that unique nugget, or that Biblical gemstone that will cause me to ooh and aah for a while.

This is the kind of message the filet steak-eating Christians appreciate. But sometimes they are so overfed on this spiritual diet that a simple message bores them. Once they have learned the basics, they have little desire to sit at God's table and be reminded of the same old things they already know. Mature Christians love to learn new truth. And for me personally, the deeper we dig into the Word, the more I enjoy it.

However, I finally reached the point, after thousands of hours of asking God, "Where's the beef? Give it to me," that I became weary of studying so much. Even the Bible says that much study will weary the flesh (Eccl. 12:12).

Then I was ruined when the Holy Spirit told me to begin ministering to youth. He directed me to a project to reach young Believers, as there is a clear lack of spiritual fathers in this generation. Why was I ruined? Because these spiritual children do not have any preconceived ideas about worship, and they love the simple preaching and teaching of the Bible. They never sit in the congregation with an attitude that they are experts who will release a rating on the message from a scale of one to ten, following the dismissal prayer. It is that childlike faith that radiates from within the young people that is so refreshing. They love to hear stories of the faith told with an inspiration of the Holy Spirit, and the faith-building events in the lives of other Believers.

TELL ME A STORY

From the time our daughter could understand stories until she was nine years of age, I developed a nightly custom with her when I was not on the road ministering. When it was time for her to go to bed, she would lie down on my left arm and say, "Tell me a story, Daddy." I asked her for the theme; would it be a story about me, mommy, her brother, or her grandparents?

After selecting the theme, story time would begin. I would paint the best picture possible and take her back through her imagination to when I grew up, when I met her mommy, when her brother was born, and the dream I had of her twelve years before she was born. That was her favorite. The stories caught her attention.

As you know, most of the teaching Jesus did was accomplished with stories called parables. Paul used his testimony—his personal conversion story—on numerous occasions as a central message that revealed the power of the Gospel.

One night after our daughter fell asleep, I began to realize that many of the world's most effective evangelists who preached God's Word also used stories to illustrate their points. When I was my daughter's age, my father was my pastor. In my younger years, I would pay little attention to what he was preaching until he started telling of an event from his early life or ministry. I don't remember many of Dad's messages from those years, but I do remember most of the stories.

One reason a story is effective is because people can understand and relate to it. My sister, who has occasionally been involved in politics, told me that one of the mistakes that even a qualified politician makes is to lay out a plan or answer a rebuttal and make it too complicated for the average voter to understand. Just as Christians speak their own language, so do politicians. They talk about bipartisanship, deficit reduction, and other topics that the average American either doesn't understand or doesn't care about. But mention in just a sound bite what you're going to do for Social Security and other such government programs, and you have their attention.

Despite the fact that more Americans are college educated and have an abundance of information at their fingertips, about forty percent of Americans are at or below a basic level of reading proficiency. On average, most are on a seventh grade level of understanding. This is one reason negative political campaign advertising works against an opponent. It plays on the fears of people who cannot think or reason for themselves, but let others think for them. They understand fear and manipulation. Stories are also effective.

Since many people are at a simple level of understanding, it seems that vanilla—or keeping it simple and plain—is better.

GOLIATH—AN NFL TEAM?

There is so much spiritual ignorance in this generation that even the simple stories we heard in Sunday School are unknown to most, because they have never attended church. When a group of teens was asked questions about the Bible, their answers were shocking. For example, Goliath, the giant that David slew, was thought to be the name of a team in the National Football League.

I have lost count of the number of times over the years that sincere people have said to me, "That was good message; at least the part I could understand." I once asked a well-known minister why, after only ten years, they could attract ten thousand attendees at a conference, and I have been in ministry over thirty years and still can't get four thousand at a conference. The answer was, "You are too deep." The detailed prophetic preaching and all of those word studies fly right over most people's heads.

I have often laughed and said that Joyce Meyer is an enigma, a mystery. She is the only woman I know who can pray, quote five Scriptures, tell a Bible story, talk about PMS, and have people wanting to hear more. Her secret is that everyone can understand her and relate to her. It is practical, simple teaching.

My friend who said my teaching was too deep reminded me that most of my audience is very solid spiritually, already deeply into the Word of God or hungry to learn more, and generally well-educated. We all have a call of our own that we must follow. While the comment was nice, I was still stuck somewhere at "too deep," doing a self-examination on how to be more effective. The answer was that, sometimes you have to be vanilla. It is not about staying at the basics all the time, but about keeping the teaching at a certain level of understanding. Sometimes it seems that we have allowed Christianity to become so complicated that folks are running right by the gates of heaven, unsure how they actually get in. Is it by joining the right church? Paying a certain amount of money each year? Doing some good works? Believing just the right doctrine?

JESUS IN A CHILD'S EYES

I want to see Jesus as a child would see Him, and experience that first conversion faith—that simple, childlike belief that I had when I was a participant in my mother's Sunday School class in Big Stone Gap, Virginia.

When our daughter was about three years of age, my wife had a beautiful snow globe on the dresser in the master bedroom. One day Amanda wanted to see it, so I picked it up and shook it. She moved close to the glass and stared at the image inside; it was the scene of the crucifixion with Mary at the foot of the cross. She said, "Who's that, Daddy?"

I said "Jesus."

Pointing to the woman she said, "Daddy, who is that?"

"That's his mother," I replied.

She looked closely and saw tiny red marks on the hands and the feet of Jesus. I said, "He's alive now and He's not on the cross anymore." Still intrigued by the red marks she asked, "Why does he have red marks and who hurt him?"

"He was crucified by mean men and He died, but He's alive today."

She said something that touched me. Pointing to Jesus inside that snow globe, she asked, "Does it still hurt, Daddy?"

I was about to reply, "No sweetheart, it doesn't hurt any more," when I was checked in my spirit. I was stirred when I heard that still, small inner voice say, "It does still hurt. It hurts when one of my children turns their back on me after I have purchased them with my own life. It hurts when one of my children will not forgive another one in my family, when I have forgiven them. It hurts when my own children do not believe that my shed blood can bring healing to them. Yes, at times it still hurts!"

It was through the eyes of a child that my own eyes were opened. I never thought about how He still hurts, but a little three-year-old girl was concerned about the hurts of Jesus.

A MARKETING BLUNDER

Go back for a moment to the opening story in this book about Coca Cola. Coke at one time made a mistake that almost cost them their reputation and product. Someone inside of Coke's office noticed that Pepsi, their competitor, was reaching out to the younger generation. Coke, to some, represented the older soda drinker and Pepsi was the choice of a "new generation." The new marketing idea was to create a new Coke.

So in 1985, the company reformulated the old Coke and introduced it as new Coke. It was a marketing disaster, and the public outcry was so strong that the company received over four hundred thousand calls on a special phone line for comments. Coke hired psychiatrists to listen in, as people were talking like it was the death of a loved one. Coke returned the old formula under the name Classic Coke. The greatest complaints against the new Coke came from Southerners who had grown up with the old Coke. To them, it was part of their culture—like barbecued ribs and college football.

The formula for Coke is simple, but it works. And if simple works, then leave simple alone and let simple work. The same is true with the message of the good news of Jesus Christ and the teaching of the Bible. It is simple. Yet, adults want to change the simple that works, and complicate the issues so that few people understand the message anymore.

Faith is not complicated. It means to believe the truth and accept the truth. Just like with Coke, it is a brand that has maintained a global reputation. Many other brand names are globally recognized—Mercedes Benz, Delta Airlines, Nike, various food and beverage franchises, and so on. But the greatest name is Jesus, and it is faith in Him and His name that has branded about 2.2 billion people as Christians, and many of these Christians discovered Jesus when they were only a child. All it took was childlike faith. Simplicity is not boring, as long as the simple thing is enjoyable. Just like with Coke, it is a brand that has maintained its global reputation for many years, because people like the taste of this same product that has been passed on for generations. The Gospel message is simple, but the story is never boring. God became man through a virgin's womb, crushed the kingdom of Satan with the authority of His words, and conquered death and hell through His death and resurrection. It is simple, but dynamic; basic, yet deep; easy-to-understand, yet life-changing.

Nothing is more refreshing than a drink from the well of living water. Nothing is more enjoyable than sitting at God's table, devouring heavenly manna being served by anointed ministers. Nothing is more life-changing than entering into a redemptive covenant with Christ! If children can understand that "Jesus loves me, this I know," then adults should believe, "for the Bible tells me so."

It is just that simple, and as easy to build a spiritual relationship with Jesus as it is for a child to build a snowman.

CHAPTER 14

CHILDREN NEED SOMEONE TO TRUST

There is A four-letter word that is whispered often, but rarely spoken aloud. It is the one experience that people have in common globally, and the one word we seldom like to admit we have. That word is *fear*. We waste many of our allotted earthly days dealing with it.

We may spend our childhood dreaming and thinking about tomorrow, but once fear whispers in our ear, it becomes increasingly difficult to see beyond the moment. Instead of looking wistfully up at the clouds, wondering what the future holds, we adults tend to lie awake at night, staring at the ceiling, and dreading the inevitable blare of the alarm clock.

Fear is another four-letter word that should be banned from our spiritual vocabulary. It turns dreams into doubt, snowmen into slush, and our confidence in God's daily bread into a scramble to avoid life's daily dread. Fear will always step in the moment we choose to let faith go. Fear and faith are equally powerful. They are two sides of the same coin. Both make the imaginable tangible. It takes as much effort to spend the spiritual currency of faith as it does to splurge on the currency of fear. It comes down to this: which piper do you want to pay? And, the spiritual law is that you always get what you give.

Look at it this way. If faith is the substance of things hoped for (Heb. 11:1), then fear is the substance of things dreaded. Faith sees hope and fear crushes hope. When a doctor diagnoses his patient with a rare disease and says it is treatable, then hope breeds faith. If he reports that there is no cure, fear often shuts the door on faith.

If faith is a substance, then fear is a substance. Both reach out and create evidence of something unseen. Medical doctors say that fear can create symptoms that mimic an actual sickness, and the mind tricks the body into believing it has the disease.

Fear is rooted in a dread of separation. Fear comes when we are afraid of a disease that could kill us, or a job that might end and bring loss of income, or a marriage in which our companion will walk out and take our security with them. We have fear of separation from something. If you submit to fear, you give substance to the very thing you dread. Faith is rooted in trust.

Most children have a trust instinct. As a child, unless you tell them not to, they will often walk up to a smiling and friendly stranger and allow the person to pick them up or hand them candy and a toy. As children we trust; as adults our disappointments in people cause us to put up walls to prevent hurt and rejection.

THE INVISIBLE MEANS OF SUPPORT

Norman, a young reporter, was assigned to cover a terrible catastrophe. Apparently a leaky gas line had ignited a multi-story apartment building, blowing away a large section of the occupied building.

Standing behind a police barricade, Norman shaded his face from the heat and watched in horror as many of the panicked residents chose to jump, rather than be consumed by the roaring flames. Trying to maintain his composure amid the confusion of sirens and screams, the young reporter flipped open his steno pad and began to write. Just as he attempted to focus on his scribbling, a single voice broke through the flames, catching Norman's ear. *"Please, somebody help me! Come and get me! Somebody, hurry please!"*

"Listen to me!" a man called from out of a window close by. "I can't get to you, Mary. This board won't support both of us. But you can come to me."

The board the man spoke of was nothing but a plank that had haphazardly fallen across the alley between the apartments and neighboring building. "All you have to do," he called out, "is crawl out on the board. C'mon!"

The anxious reporter could see the man's outstretched arms motioning to the young girl, but she would not budge.

"I can't, I'll fall! Please somebody come get me!"

As Norman watched, now oblivious to his pen and pad, a section of debris broke loose and fell with a crash dangerously near the stranded girl. Instantly, without consciously thinking, the reporter handed the tools of his trade to a bystander and jumped the police barricade. Fixing his eyes on the young girl, Norman zigzagged his way through a maze of scurrying firemen until he reached the closest possible location to the girl.

Norman cupped his hands to his mouth and shouted, "Don't look down, just listen."

"Please," the girl screamed across to the man in the next window, "come get me!"

"There is no one over there who can help you, Mary. But there is someone with you who can!"

"There is nobody up here," the girl whimpered, looking down at Norman.

"Yes there is, Mary. God is up there with you. He is holding out His hand. He won't let you fall!"

"I can't! I can't!"

"Yes, you can! God is waiting to help you. But you've got to work with Him. He put that board there is for you. He meant for you to use it."

Clinging desperately to the shaky wall, the youngster remained immovable and continued to cry.

"Mary, believe me," Norman called out in earnest, "God is there with you. He told you so Himself. He said, 'I am with you always.' That means NOW!"

As the reporter confidently spoke, Mary's rigid, frightened body slowly relaxed and began to move.

"That's it, you're doing fine," he coached. "Now, crawl out on the board. It's the escape God provided. It's good, strong, and plenty wide."

As she grasped the board, feeling its weight and thickness, the youngster froze once again. "I can't."

"Think Mary. If the board was on the ground, you could cross it with your eyes shut. So close your eyes. Use your imagination—and go!"

In slow motion, the young girl edged onto the board, her eyes shut tight. The plank creaked and bowed under her weight, but the wooden span refused to buckle.

Cupping his hands to his face again, Norman shouted, "Just keep saying to yourself, 'With God's help I can do it. With God's help I can do it. With God's help I am doing it. God and I are doing it!' "

Suspended above the alley, her trembling voice began to repeat each line, "With God's help I can do it. With God's help I am doing it!" Inching slowly but surely across the breach, her voice grew stronger. "God and I are doing it."

Finally, as Norman peered up through the smoky haze, a pair of strong arms appeared in the window and took hold of the youngster's small frame.

"You did it, Mary!" the young reporter leaped and shouted. "You and God did it!"

After basking a moment in the joy of the rescue, Norman gathered himself. Remembering his assignment, he made his way back to the police barricade to retrieve his pad and pen. There, a bystander patted him on the back and smiled. "Hey, nice goin' out there. You're some preacher."

Quickly turning to face the man, the young reporter shook his head and replied, "I'm not a preacher."

Shrugging his shoulders, the bystander raised an eyebrow and countered, "Well, you should be, mister. You should be."

The man's words echoed in the reporter's ears for weeks, prompting countless memories of his childhood days as a rebellious pastor's son. In time the young man realized he could no longer fight it; he knew the bystander was right. And finally, one fateful day, upon whispering, "With God's help, I can do it," young Norman Vincent Peale laid down his pad and pen and picked up a Bible to become one of America's noted ministers.

Saving one child inspired this journalist to save others. Trust is built upon confidence in a person's words and actions. For the average child, it takes little prodding before they will trust someone. For an adult, life's disappointments can create a trust crisis. When a husband walks out for another woman, when a friend reveals a secret that was sealed between the two of you, or when the car repairman ripped you off, the walls of mistrust rise.

One of my spiritual daughters shared with me how, as a teenager, she became enamored with a football player and became emotionally attached to him, to the point she was willing to leave home and move to the state where he was moving, feeling certain she would marry him. She discovered, however, that he was a two-timing fellow and had another girl on the string.

She was so disheartened and despondent that she surrounded herself with mental walls, only allowing two men—her dad and her brother—into her life. This one betrayal emptied out her trust bank. Through prayer, she restored her own self-confidence and confidence in others, knowing that people fail, but God never will.

Children need someone they can trust, and so do adults. There is a friend that sticks closer than a brother (Prov. 18:24), and He will rescue you from the fire and bring you to safety. His name is Jesus.

CHAPTER 15

CHILDLIKE, BUT NOT CHILDISH

This chapter BRINGS us to an important topic—the difference between being childlike and childish. Children are little people trapped in a small body, with immature thoughts and childish manners. In this book I have shared with you how children can teach us certain things about faith, love, and intimacy with God.

Too often, however, instead of maintaining a childlike simplicity in Christ, believers become childish. They fuss over petty things and become territorial like a bully on a playground. The church should never become the town's adult nursery, where Papa Pastor is required to change the members' diapers, hand out pacifiers, and spend precious time burping and affirming his spoiled adult children.

When Paul wrote 1 Corinthians 13, a chapter in our Bible that deals with love, he penned these words:

> *"When I was a child, I spake as a child, I understood as a child, I thought as a child: but when I became a man, I put away childish things."*
>
> *—1 Corinthians 13:11 (KJV)*

This is the only place in the English translation where the word *childish* is used. The Greek word here is *nepios*, and it can mean an infant, or figuratively, a simple-minded person who acts immature. Notice that Paul spoke of being childish and not childlike. There is a difference. Jesus said:

"Assuredly, I say to you, whoever does not receive the kingdom of God as a little child will by no means enter it. And He took them up in His arms, put His hands on them, and blessed them."
—Mark 10:15-16 (NKJV)

Scholars have pondered what Christ meant when he spoke of receiving the kingdom as a little child. Receiving the kingdom begins by believing the message of the kingdom. The kingdom is *received* (by repenting and being converted - Matt. 18:3) and this is the first process that leads a person into *entering* the kingdom. Christ called the children "little ones" (Matt. 10:42; 18:6; 18:14). The Greek phrase is *mikros*, which means *small in size or number.* Mistreating the little ones is so serious that Christ issued a warning to anyone who would offend a little one who believed on Him, when He said that it would be better that you have a millstone tied around your neck and be drowned in the sea, than to offend a little one (Matt. 18:6).

How does an adult become as a child and receive the kingdom and all of its blessings? I believe the answer is found in the summary of what has been written in this book:

- A child can believe that nothing is impossible.

- A child can imagine that something they cannot see will become something that they can see.

- A child knows how to express affection and desires the attention of his or her parents.

- A child loves unconditionally and can get along with other children without pretense or the need for a résumé.

In summary, believing is easy for a child. And believing in God, His promises, and His blessings should be easy and normal for a Believer of any age.

The one thing, however, that will hinder the kingdom is when that *child in you* moves from being *childlike* to *childish*. We brag on our children when they are polite, kind, gentle, disciplined and obedient. When they are rude, mean, impolite and disobedient, we call them childish. We enter the kingdom as a babe in Christ, through a pure and sincere faith. Then too often, we become an adult and our childlikeness turns into childishness.

When you don't get the color of carpet you wanted in the Sunday School room at church and begin to pout about it, then you are acting childish. If you were replaced by another singer doing a solo in the choir and you are offended at the choir director, you are being childish. If the pastor walked by and didn't speak or stroke your ego by expressing his appreciation for your hard work, and you suddenly develop a negative attitude, you are acting like a child on the playground who was not invited to the swing set with the others kids. Get over it.

Most church problems are not spiritual conflicts and have nothing to do with demonic spirits, satanic assignments, or evil strategies laid out by the kingdom of darkness. They are caused by *emotions gone wild,* provoked by overactive imaginations and opposing opinions, all of which collide with egos. This empowers the planting of seeds of confusion, envy, strife, and offense. At times the devil gets blamed for a church split, and his agents weren't even stalking the neighborhood when two Believers came out swinging swords, leaving a field of wounded in their path. It might not be the devil at all; it might be you!

The real enemy was actually your *inner me,* or that carnal nature dueling with your spiritual one. If the sinners would *confess up*, the backsliders would *get back up*, the saints withholding tithe would *pay up,* and the immature Christians would *grow up,* then we wouldn't have as many *blow ups* that could hinder you one day from *going up*!

Jesus said:

> *"Therefore whoever humbles himself as this little child is the greatest in the kingdom of heaven. Whoever receives one little child like this in My name receives Me."*
> —*Matthew 18:4-5 (NKJV)*

Years ago I heard the story of a minister who lived to be in his 90s. Throughout his lifetime he had journeyed far and near, making converts for the Kingdom, along with a host of friendships. In his seventies and eighties, he still had the zeal, the fire, and the inner strength to preach the Gospel. He was energetic and excited, and he preached each message with such an anointing and motivation that it could be his last.

When asked how, through many years of ministry he continually re-fired instead of retired, he made this statement, *"The Gospel never lost its wonder."*

What did he mean, its wonder? It was the wonder of a message that can snatch a soul from the pit of destruction, and the wonder of the anointing that takes a common man and makes him speak the oracles of God.

The early church experienced miracles, signs, and wonders (Heb. 2:4). Some churches teach that we no longer need the signs because we now have the Bible. The same group theorizes that miracles are no longer nec-essary, as we have doctors, medicine, and other methods to cure sickness and disease. For these Christians who doubt God's miraculous ability, I label them unbelieving Believers. Their church services are dry because they have rejected the miraculous signs, and that causes them to lose the wonders. The only wonder on a Sunday morning are the spiritually dead members who wonder what time the service will end.

In the eyes of a child, life is filled with wonders. There is the amaze-ment of a colorful butterfly darting between the flowers, or the baby birds that are discovered in a back yard nest. There is the wonder of dis-covering sea shells on a beach, and the beauty of a sunset. Then there is snow. In Davis, West Virginia, when the winter blizzards blanketed the town with snow, and the trees were covered with snow and ice that shim-mered like crystals, I called it a winter wonderland. This is why a child can *make* a snowman and *believe* it is alive in their *imagination.* This is why they jump and dance while being dusted with heaven's snowflakes, no two of which are alike.

Such beauty is not a sign, and we certainly see no supernatural miracle involved. But it is a *wonder.* Never let your Heavenly Father, the Holy Spirit, the Son Jesus Christ, and the Word of the Lord lose its wonder. And now and then, never forget how to dance with a snowman.

CHAPTER 16

CHILDREN NEVER DREAD WINTER AND NEITHER SHOULD WE

Human life cycles are parallel to the four seasons of the year: the spring of newness and youth; then the summer of growth and maturity; the fall of harvesting, after seeds of past work have matured into the fruit of present blessings; and finally, the cool, dreary days of winter.

My wife and I anticipate the arrival of fall, when the burning heat of August turns to the refreshing winds of September and the coolness and beauty of October. One October, we drove from our home to Pigeon Forge, Tennessee to view the change of the leaves in the heart of Tennessee's Smokey Mountains. God had stroked His paintbrush across the rugged mountains and splashed reds, oranges, and yellows across the forests.

Driving back home, I observed trees along the interstate highway that had already lost their leaves. The strong winds had plucked the colorful foliage off their branches, one leaf at a time, leaving the skeleton of what had been. One naked tree even looked like a skeleton, seemingly with twisted arms reaching up to heaven and crying out for help. As a visual person with an energized imagination, that's one thing I dislike about winter—the deciduous trees are now stripped of their coverings and are a barren reminder of a previous, more appealing season.

It is these trees that remind me of the winter that arrives in the life of every person on earth. Two men who had the greatest impact on my life were my grandfather, John Bava, and my father, Fred Stone. Besides pastoring a church and being involved in other entrepreneurial endeavors, Granddad wrote, published, and recorded Gospel music. My father was the greatest praying man I had ever known, and he operated in all the spiritual gifts.

I was in Africa ministering when Granddad was taken into surgery and never left the hospital alive. Dad lived a strong, healthy life until he reached his mid-seventies. During the last two years in the life of this man of great faith, he suffered from kidney failure and began to lose his eyesight. His final week was spent in hospice care in a nursing home facility.

About five months before his death, I was talking to him about how life moves in seasons. He knew that he was in the final throes of the winter of his life. Dad was seated in the passenger seat when I pulled into his driveway. I asked, "What do you think it will be like when you die? Do you ever think about it?" He paused and stared out the window to a tree with its colorful leaves falling on the ground. Then he turned and said, "I believe it will be a glorious departure!"

Fred Stone was not afraid of winter, and he was not afraid of death.

In nature, everything slows down in winter. The warm air turns to cold wind and we dread heading outdoors to face the shock of bitter temperatures as we crank up the car. The house must be heated to a comfortable level, and we spend more time in front of a television with a blanket draped over ourselves for additional comfort. Sleep comes easier in the winter. At times we feel like a bear huddled in a cave, just wanting to hibernate to avoid what is outside of our warm cave. At dinner we are satisfied with a bowl of warm soup, and we exchange summer drinks for hot chocolate. The natural and spiritual realms both have their seasons of winter.

When age and time collide and our countdown clock to eternity begins to tick, a lifetime of special events and family vacations to our favorite beach or mountain cabin become a memory lost in the fog of forgetfulness. Our weary mind might forget important events and focus instead on the coming exit from this life to the next. Or perhaps our mind may relive memories like a rerun of a favorite movie, but our body shocks us back to reality, reminding us that our future is short and time is ticking down. We know that whatever images we can capture on the worn-out computer of our mind, we should enjoy while we can.

For many people, including some Believers, winter can be a somber, almost depressing time. Like low black clouds and the distant thunder of an oncoming storm, the hoof beats of the rider of the death echo across the valley with an arrow marked with your name.

However, winter doesn't have to be all that bad, because this is the season that occurs just before the coming spring. For a Believer, what ends on earth in winter initiates a new spring in the heavenly paradise of God (2 Cor. 12:1-4).

Here on earth, the natural season of winter comes every year, and older folks might not enjoy the thoughts of winter. But there is one group that looks forward to the occasion, because of the fun they enjoy during this season. The skies of winter may appear dreary, but the white snow replaces the dull moods with sleds, snowmen, snowball fights, and unrestrained outdoor activities.

Remember your mother saying, "Bundle up and don't get wet. You might catch a cold"? Are you kidding? Have you ever heard a child say to another child, "Don't get that snow on me. I might catch a cold." Or, "Don't throw me in the snow; it might make my nose run." Of course not; only adults worry about the cold wet snow.

Adults view winter and snow as something that adds more cares to life. They have to heat up the car, shovel snow off the driveway, and bundle up in heavy coats. But to a child, this is interpreted as *fun*!

Looking at winter in the spiritual sense, how can this season be exciting for an adult, knowing you are at the end of your cycle of life on earth? If you are not a Believer, it is certainly a dreaded occasion with nothing positive to look forward to. You will be separated from family as you are separated from God. Without a redemptive covenant in Christ, the eternal future is bleak and dark. However, for a Believer, imagine what the close of winter brings! It means you have finished your race and are about to cross the finish line and see the face of your Redeemer. When you cross the finish line and enter the gate of eternal life, you will be reunited with the departed souls of loved ones who died in Christ. Waiting for you will be an entire city prepared from the foundation of the world. In the kingdom of God, the last season of your earthly life introduces the heavenly spring season of newness.

Winter is about perception. I have heard people who are months away from their earthly departure say that getting old is a curse, and they hate getting old. Others will say, "Well, it won't be long and I won't have to suffer in this old beat up body anymore. My pains and aches will be over and I'll have a new body." Winter is a separation from loved ones that they will not see again for many years. But others see winter as an opportunity to go to heaven before the rest of their family members, and wait for their arrival one day in the future.

When my precious father was in a Life Care facility the final days of his life, he was unable to eat or drink. During those days, I was blessed on a couple of occasions to stay up with him the entire night. As he lay there suffering in his body, I would begin to sing many of the old hymns, to which, with eyes closed, he would begin to slowly nod his head.

One night, three days before he passed away, the room was dark with the exception of a small lamp on a table. At about one o'clock in the morning, I was overwhelmed with an intense desire to pray. I began interceding, quietly at first, but as a spiritual fire ignited in my spirit, my words became louder. My words were flowing to God and suddenly turned into a prophetic type of thanksgiving prayer, in which I began to recall the life and ministry of my dad, from age seventeen to the very end. In my entire ministry, that one hour alone with dad, who was on his death bed, was the most glorious hour I have ever experienced as we were engulfed in the Divine Presence of God. I felt as though angels were assigned at the doors and were waiting for a heavenly signal to release Dad's spirit from his weak body. This Divinely charged atmosphere entered the room of a dying man, in the last days of his winter season.

On Friday the moment arrived when earth and heaven were preparing to kiss, and through the kiss of death Dad's spirit left his sick body and entered his heavenly home. Before his death, his lungs began to fill with fluid and his breathing became shallow and difficult. It reminded me of my wife when she was in labor with our children, as she breathed hard and fast to deal with the pain of childbirth. I heard this thought: We enter this world with birth pains and we leave with similar pains of death.

Dad's physical suffering would soon end and his eternal soul and spirit would be released. In the same manner, at the peak of labor pains, a child is released from the womb and begins a new life of its own.

There are two ways in which a Believer can transfer from earth to heaven—either through the return of Christ (1 Thess. 4:16-17) or through death. Most Believers would prefer the first over the latter. Those who are alive at the return of Christ will be the only generation of Believers in history who will escape the winter season of life and the darkness of the future great tribulation. For those who will ride with the angel of death, the darkness of winter will melt when the brightness of the heavenly city comes into view. Their winter will become an eternal spring. Earth will be the final winter you will ever encounter.

There is a tombstone that reads: I have been where you have been, and you are going where I am. If this were on my grave marker, I would say it this way:

> I have been where you are
> You will be where I am
> Until then serve God, love people, enjoy life
> I'll see you when your winter is over

When winter comes, there is something wonderful to look forward to. Like children who don't dread winter, neither should we. Let the grace of God empower you to keep dancing with your snowman, up to the very end!

NOTES

Chapter 1

1. The History of Coca Cola,
http://inventors.about.com/od/cstartinventions/a/coca_cola.htm
(accessed August 21, 2103

2. History, *The Legend of St. Nicholas*,
http://www.history.com/topics/santa-claus (accessed August 21, 2013)

3. St. Nicholas Center, *Who is St. Nicholas?*,
http://www.stnicholascenter.org/pages/who-is-st-nicholas/
(accessed August 21, 2013)

4. Coca Cola Journey, *The True History of the Modern Day Santa Claus*,
http://www.coca-colacompany.com/stories/coke-lore-santa-claus
(accessed August 21, 2013)

5. When is Hanukkah (Chanukah) on the Hebrew calendar and the
secular calendar?
http://www.chabad.org/holidays/chanukah/article_cdo/aid/671899/jewish/
When-is-Hanukkah-Chanukah-in-2012-2013-2014-and-2015.htm

6. Ronald L. Eisenberg, *Jewish Traditions*
(Philadelphia: The Jewish Publication Society, 2008), 244